Reasoning and Writing

Level B
Writing Extensions

A Division of The McGraw-Hill Companies

Columbus, Ohio

Cover Credits

(t) Photo Spin, (b) PhotoDisc.

Illustration Credit

Susan Jerde

SRA/McGraw-Hill

A Division of The McGraw-Hill Companies

Copyright © 2001 by SRA/McGraw-Hill.

Send all inquiries to:
SRA/McGraw-Hill
8787 Orion Place
Columbus, OH 43240-4027

Printed in the United States of America.

ISBN 0-02-684767-1

3 4 5 6 7 8 9 PBM 06 05 04 03 02

Contents

Introduction

Writing Extensions, Level B

The writing extensions for the second-grade level of *Reasoning and Writing* consist of 60 scripted lessons (lessons 1–60 in this book) and 56 blackline masters (BLMs) for specified lessons.

Scheduling the Extension Activities

Each extension lesson takes 10–30 minutes. Start the extensions by presenting lesson 1 and presenting the lessons in order. Present at least 5 extension lessons a week. After students have completed *Reasoning and Writing*, Level B, present at least 10 extension lessons a week.

You may start the extension materials when the children have completed lesson 50 of *Reasoning and Writing*, Level B. Note that the extension activities should not replace any regular lessons in *Reasoning and Writing*.

Do not start the materials as early as lesson 51 of *Reasoning and Writing* unless the children are firm on all activities in the *Reasoning and Writing* lessons. Also, make sure that they are able to write at least 8 words per minute. If they are not firm, practice the skills in which they are weak and delay the introduction of *Writing Extensions*, Level B, until after they complete *Reasoning and Writing*, Level B. Then present the extensions at the rate of one or two per day.

Objectives

The writing extensions have the following objectives:

1. To provide children with practice in completing and composing sentences that follow a particular pattern;

2. To increase the children's rate and facility at writing single sentences and groups of sentences on lined paper;
3. To give children practice in expressing the main idea and supporting details shown in a picture or group of pictures;
4. To give children practice in reporting on the actions shown in picture sequences;
5. To give children practice in describing how to make two things that are different the same;
6. To give children practice in describing the steps in a how-to process;
7. To give children practice in writing and illustrating finished works (writing both rough draft and final draft and then illustrating the report);
8. To permit children to express personal preferences and report on personal experiences.

Using the Teacher Presentation Scripts

The script conventions for the extension lessons are the same as those for *Reasoning and Writing*. The teaching practices are also the same. For information about these practices, refer to the Teacher's Guide for *Reasoning and Writing*.

Procedures for Presenting Lessons

The teacher presentation script for each lesson specifies the blackline master for the lesson. The number of the blackline master corresponds to the extension lesson number. For extension lesson 3 you will use BLM 3.

You may either duplicate the BLM and provide each child with a copy or make an overhead of the BLM and display it to the entire group.

Children will need lined paper for all 60 lessons and materials for illustrating their last four reports (extension lessons 57–60).

Tracks

Writing Parallel Sentences

In extension lessons 1–41, children write parallel sentences. The picture on the BLM shows two characters that are parallel in some way. You first direct children to copy the sentence that tells about one character. Then they write a parallel sentence that tells about the other character. Here's the BLM for lesson 7.

The children copy the sentence about a cat. Then they write a parallel sentence about a dog.

In later activities, no sentences are given. In extension lessons 48–52, children write a sentence that tells the "main idea" that describes both characters in the picture. Then they write a parallel sentence for each character. The parallel sentences are specific. These activities therefore give children practice in creating main ideas and supporting detail.

Note that this type of practice is ideal for increasing writing rate and for giving children the idea that they are to write the way they talk. They are not to think about a word at a time but rather to think about the pattern of words that they are going to produce.

Reporting on an Illustrated Sequence

Children base what they will write on a sequence of either three or four pictures. Initially, they describe the main thing that happened in each picture. Here's an example of lesson 42.

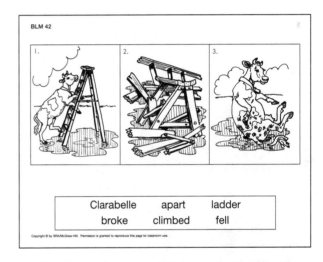

For the first picture, children start with the name **Clarabelle** and tell what she did in the first picture. For the next picture, they start with the words **the ladder** and tell what the ladder did when Clarabelle climbed it. For picture 3, children write a sentence that tells what happened to Clarabelle.

In later exercises, children compose a sentence that tells about all the pictures in the sequence (the main-idea sentence). Then they write a sentence about each of the pictures.

Here's an example from lesson 54.

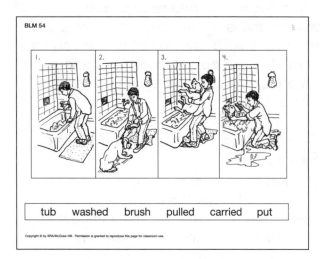

Children first write a sentence that tells what the boy did: The boy washed his dog. Then they write about the specific things the boy did to wash the dog, starting with a sentence that tells about the first picture: The boy filled the bathtub with water.

Writing Directions About Making Two Things the Same

The BLMs for these exercises show two similar things. Children tell about how to change one of the things so it becomes identical to the other thing. Here's the BLM for lesson 44.

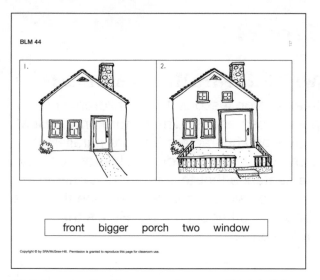

Children write three sentences that tell how to change house one so it looks just like house two.

Writing About Personal Experiences

Starting with lesson 57, children write about personal experiences. They are given a title, such as **A Time I Was Really Scared.** Children write sentences that tell about when, where, why and what happened. They are encouraged to tell about what happened later on and how they feel about the incident now. All these accounts are written first as rough drafts, then as final drafts and finally as "published" or displayed works that are accompanied with illustrations.

Extension Lessons
Table of Contents

Extension Lesson 1

Materials: BLM 1. Lined paper.

Objective: **Compose and write a parallel sentence pair based on a single picture.**

WRITING PARALLEL SENTENCES

1. (Display or hand out BLM 1. Point to the picture.)
   You're going to write about this picture on your lined paper.
2. The picture shows what the cat and the dog were doing. The cat and the dog were sitting. One of them was sitting in the grass. Which animal was that? (Signal.) *The cat.*
 * Where was the dog sitting? (Call on a child. Idea: *On the chair.*)

3. (Point to the first sentence below the picture.)
   The first sentence is written and part of the next sentence is written.
 * The first sentence says: **The cat was sitting in the grass.** Everybody, say that sentence. (Signal.) *The cat was sitting in the grass.*
 * The second sentence should say: **The dog was sitting on the chair.** Say that sentence. (Signal.) *The dog was sitting on the chair.*
4. I'll say the first sentence. You tell me what the second sentence should say.
 * **The cat was sitting in the grass.** Tell me about the dog. (Signal.) *The dog was sitting on the chair.*
5. Look at your lined paper. ✔
 * The line that goes up and down is the margin. What is the up-and-down line? (Signal.) *The margin.*
 * Here's the rule about the margin: You start writing words just after the margin. Where do you start writing words? (Signal.) *Just after the margin.*
 * Now copy the first sentence just as it's written below the picture. Remember, start the sentence just after the margin. Begin the sentence with a capital **T.** Don't write capital letters anywhere except at the beginning of the sentence. Put a period at the end of the sentence. Raise your hand when you're finished with the first sentence.
   (Observe children and give feedback.)

6. (Write on the board:)

chair	on

- Here are words you'll need: chair . . . on. Spell them correctly in your second sentence. Copy and complete the second sentence. Remember to start with a capital letter and put a period at the end of the sentence. Begin your sentence just after the margin.

(Observe children and give feedback. Praise children with specific comments such as:) Good starting with a capital; good starting just before the margin; good spelling; good putting a period at the end of the sentence.

7. Skip a line on your paper and write both sentences again. Write: The cat was sitting in the grass. The dog was sitting on the chair.

(Observe children and give feedback.)

Extension Lesson 2

Materials: BLM 2. Lined paper.	
Objective: Compose and write a parallel sentence pair based on a single picture.	

WRITING PARALLEL SENTENCES

1. (Display or hand out BLM 2. Point to the picture.)
   You're going to write about this picture on your lined paper.

2. The picture shows what the dog and the cat were doing. The dog and the cat were sitting. One of them was sitting on the table. Which animal was that? (Signal.) *The cat.*

   • Where was the dog sitting? (Signal.) *On the floor.*

3. (Point to the first sentence below the picture.)
   The first sentence is written and part of the next sentence is written.

   • The first sentence says: **The dog was sitting on the floor.** Say that sentence. (Signal.) *The dog was sitting on the floor.*

   • The second sentence should say: **The cat was sitting on the table.** Say that sentence. (Signal.) *The cat was sitting on the table.*

4. I'll say the first sentence. You tell me what the second sentence should say.

   • **The dog was sitting on the floor.** Tell me about the cat. (Signal.) *The cat was sitting on the table.*

5. (Write on the board:)

table

   • Here's a word you'll need: table. Spell it correctly in your sentence.

   • Write both sentences on your lined paper. Copy the sentence that is written and complete the second sentence. Remember to start both sentences with a capital letter and put a period at the end of each sentence. (Observe children and give feedback.)

6. Skip a line on your paper and write both sentences again. Write: The dog was sitting on the floor. The cat was sitting on the table.
   (Observe children and give feedback.)

WRITING PARALLEL SENTENCES

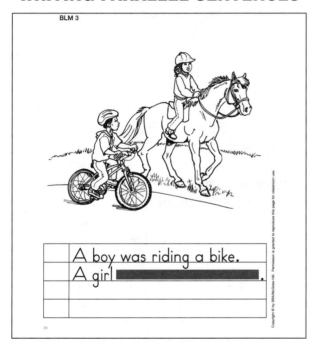

1. (Display or hand out BLM 3. Point to the picture.)
   You're going to write about this picture.
2. The picture shows what a boy and a girl were doing. They were both riding something. One of them was riding a bike. Who was that? (Signal.) *The boy.*
 • What was the girl riding? (Signal.) *A horse.*

3. (Point to the first sentence below the picture.)
   The first sentence is written and part of the next sentence is written.
 • The first sentence says: **A boy was riding a bike.** Say that sentence. (Signal.) *A boy was riding a bike.*
 • Tell me what the second sentence should say about a girl. (Signal.) *A girl was riding a horse.*
   Yes. A girl was riding a horse.
 • Once more. Say the sentence about a boy. (Signal.) *A boy was riding a bike.*
 • Say the sentence about a girl. (Signal.) *A girl was riding a horse.*
4. (Write on the board:)

> **horse**

 • Here's a word you'll need: horse. Spell it correctly in your sentence.
 • Write both sentences on your lined paper. Copy the sentence that is written and complete the second sentence. Remember to start both sentences with a capital letter and put a period at the end of each sentence. (Observe children and give feedback.)
5. Skip a line on your paper and write both sentences again. Write: A boy was riding a bike. A girl was riding a horse. (Observe children and give feedback.)

Extension Lesson 4

> **Materials:** BLM 4. Lined paper.
>
> **Objective:** Compose and write a parallel sentence pair based on a single picture.

WRITING PARALLEL SENTENCES

1. (Display or hand out BLM 4. Point to the picture.)
   You're going to write about this picture.
2. The picture shows what a girl and a boy did. They rode something. One of them rode an elephant. Who was that? (Signal.) *The girl.*
   - What did the boy ride? (Signal.) *A bike.*

3. (Point to the first sentence below the picture.)
   The first sentence is written and part of the second sentence is written.
   - The first sentence says: **The girl rode an elephant.** Say that sentence. (Signal.) *The girl rode an elephant.*
   - Tell me what the second sentence should say about the boy. (Signal.) *The boy rode a bike.*
     Yes. The boy rode a bike.
   - Once more. Say the sentence about the girl. (Signal.) *The girl rode an elephant.*
   - Say the sentence about the boy. (Signal.) *The boy rode a bike.*
4. (Write on the board:)

bike

   - Here's a word you'll need: bike. Spell it correctly in your sentence.
   - Write both sentences on your lined paper. Remember to start with a capital letter and put a period at the end of each sentence.
     (Observe children and give feedback.)
5. Skip a line on your paper and write both sentences again.
   (Observe children and give feedback.)

Extension Lesson 5

Materials: BLM 5. Lined Paper.

Objective: Compose and write a parallel sentence pair based on a single picture.

WRITING PARALLEL SENTENCES

1. (Display or hand out BLM 5. Point to the picture.)
   You're going to write about this picture.
2. The picture shows what a boy and a girl did. They read something. One of them read a paper. Who was that? (Signal.) *The boy.*

- What did the girl read? (Signal.) *A book.*
3. Look at the sentence.
   The sentence says: **The boy read a paper.** Say that sentence. (Signal.) *The boy read a paper.*
- Tell me what the second sentence should say about the girl. (Signal.) *The girl read a book.*
- Once more. Say the sentence about the boy. (Signal.) *The boy read a paper.*
- Say the sentence about the girl. (Signal.) *The girl read a book.*
4. (Write on the board:)

book

- Here's a word you'll need: book.
- Write both sentences. Remember to start with a capital letter and put a period at the end of each sentence. (Observe children and give feedback.)
5. Skip a line on your paper and write both sentences again. (Observe children and give feedback.)

Extension Lesson 5 **13**

Extension Lesson 6

Materials: BLM 6. Lined paper.	
Objective: Compose and write a parallel sentence pair based on a single picture.	

WRITING PARALLEL SENTENCES

1. (Display or hand out BLM 6. Point to the picture.)
   You're going to write about this picture.
2. The picture shows what a girl and a boy were doing.
   • Where was the boy standing? (Signal.) *On the floor.*
   • Where was the girl standing? (Call on a child. Idea: *On a chair.*)

3. Look at the sentence.
   Everybody, say that sentence. (Signal.) *The girl was standing on a chair.*
   • Tell me what the second sentence should say about the boy. (Signal.) *The boy was standing on the floor.*
   Yes. The boy was standing on the floor.
   • Once more. Say the sentence about the girl. (Signal.) *The girl was standing on a chair.*
   • Say the sentence about the boy. (Signal.) *The boy was standing on the floor.*
4. (Write on the board:)

   floor

   • Here's a word you'll need: floor.
   • Write both sentences. Remember to start with a capital letter and put a period at the end of each sentence. (Observe children and give feedback.)
5. Skip a line on your paper and write both sentences again. (Observe children and give feedback.)

Materials: BLM 7. Lined paper.

Objective: Compose and write a parallel sentence pair based on a single picture.

WRITING PARALLEL SENTENCES

1. (Display or hand out BLM 7. Point to the picture.)
   You're going to write about this picture.
2. The picture shows what a cat and a dog were doing. What were they doing? (Signal.) *Sleeping.*
   - Where was the cat sleeping? (Call on a child. Idea: *On a chair.*)
   - Everybody, where was the dog sleeping? (Signal.) *On the floor.*

3. Look at the sentence.
   Say that sentence. (Signal.) *A cat was sleeping on the chair.*
   - Tell me what the second sentence should say about a dog. (Signal.) *A dog was sleeping on the floor.*
   - Once more. Say the sentence about a cat. (Signal.) *A cat was sleeping on the chair.*
   - Say the sentence about a dog. (Signal.) *A dog was sleeping on the floor.*
4. (Write on the board:)

chair	floor	sleeping

   - Here are some words you'll need: chair . . . floor . . . sleeping.
   - Write both sentences. Remember to start with a capital letter and put a period at the end of each sentence. (Observe children and give feedback.)
5. Skip a line on your paper and write both sentences again. (Observe children and give feedback.)

Extension Lesson 8

WRITING PARALLEL SENTENCES

1. (Display or hand out BLM 8. Point to the picture.)
   You're going to write about this picture.
2. The picture shows what a girl and a boy were doing. One of them was reading something. Who was that? (Signal.) *The boy.*
   • What was the girl doing? (Call on a child. Idea: *Drawing a picture.*)

3. Everybody, get ready to read the sentence. (Signal.) *The girl was drawing a picture.*
   • Tell me what the second sentence should say about the boy. (Signal.) *The boy was reading a book.*
   • Once more. Say the sentence about the boy. (Signal.) *The boy was reading a book.*
   • Say the sentence about the girl. (Signal.) *The girl was drawing a picture.*
4. (Write on the board:)

reading	book

   • Here are words you'll need: reading . . . book.
   • Write both sentences. Remember to start with a capital letter and put a period at the end of each sentence. (Observe children and give feedback.)
5. Skip a line on your paper and write both sentences again. (Observe children and give feedback.)

Materials: BLM 9. Lined paper.

Objective: Compose and write a parallel sentence pair based on a single picture.

WRITING PARALLEL SENTENCES

1. (Display or hand out BLM 9. Point to the picture.)
   You're going to write about this picture.
2. The picture shows what a boy and a girl did.
   • What did the boy do? (Signal.) *Peeled a banana.*
   • What did the girl do? (Call on a child. Idea: *Poured some milk.*)

3. Listen: The boy peeled a banana. The girl poured some milk.
   • Everybody, say the first sentence. (Signal.) *The boy peeled a banana.*
   • Say the next sentence. (Signal.) *The girl poured some milk.*
   (Repeat sentences until firm.)
4. Look at the vocabulary box. That's the box with the words in it. These are words that you will use when you write your sentences. I'll read the words: milk . . . poured . . . some . . . banana . . . peeled.
   These are words that you will use when you write your sentences.
5. Say the sentence about the boy. (Signal.) *The boy peeled a banana.*
   • Say the sentence about the girl. (Signal.) *The girl poured some milk.*
   • Write both sentences. Remember to start with a capital letter and end each sentence with a period.
   (Observe children and give feedback.)
6. Skip a line on your paper and write both sentences again.
   (Observe children and give feedback.)

Extension Lesson 10

Materials: BLM 10. Lined paper.

Objective: Compose and write a parallel sentence pair based on a single picture.

WRITING PARALLEL SENTENCES

Note: Remind children to start their sentences with a capital and end them with a period.

1. (Display or hand out BLM 10. Point to the picture.)
   You're going to write about this picture.

2. The picture shows what a girl and a boy did.
   - What did the girl do? (Signal.) *Peeled an orange.*
   - What did the boy do? (Call on a child. Idea: *Ate an apple.*)

3. Listen: The girl peeled an orange. The boy ate an apple.
   - Everybody, say the first sentence. (Signal.) *The girl peeled an orange.*
   - Say the next sentence. (Signal.) *The boy ate an apple.*
   (Repeat sentences until firm.)

4. Look at the vocabulary box. These are some of the words you need: an apple . . . an orange . . . peeled . . . ate.

5. Say the sentence about the girl. (Signal.) *The girl peeled an orange.*
   - Say the sentence about the boy. (Signal.) *The boy ate an apple.*
   - Write both sentences. (Observe children and give feedback.)

6. Skip a line on your paper and write both sentences again (Observe children and give feedback.)

Materials: BLM 11. Lined paper.

Objective: Compose and write a parallel sentence pair based on a single picture.

WRITING PARALLEL SENTENCES

BLM 11

standing   sitting   table   wagon

Copyright © by SRA/McGraw-Hill. Permission is granted to reproduce this page for classroom use.

Note: Remind children to start their sentences with a capital and end them with a period.

1. (Display or hand out BLM 11. Point to the picture.)
   You're going to write about this picture.

2. The picture shows what a dog and a cat were doing. One of them was standing in a wagon. Which animal was that? (Signal.) *The dog.*

3. Listen: The dog was standing in a wagon. The cat was sitting on a table.
   - Say the whole sentence about the dog. (Signal.) *The dog was standing in a wagon.*
   - Say the whole sentence about the cat. (Signal.) *The cat was sitting on a table.* (Repeat sentences until firm.)

4. Look at the vocabulary box. These are some of the words you need: standing . . . sitting . . . table . . . wagon.

5. Say the sentence about the dog. (Signal.) *The dog was standing in a wagon.*
   - Say the sentence about the cat. (Signal.) *The cat was sitting on a table.*
   - Write both sentences. (Observe children and give feedback.)

6. Skip a line on your paper and write both sentences again. (Observe children and give feedback.)

Extension Lesson 12

Materials: BLM 12. Lined paper.

Objective: Compose and write a parallel sentence pair based on a single picture.

WRITING PARALLEL SENTENCES

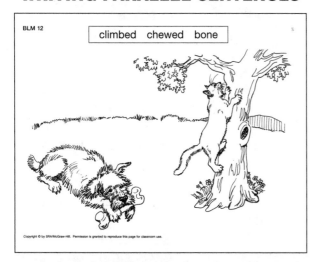

Note: Remind children to start their sentences with a capital and end them with a period.

1. (Display or hand out BLM 12. Point to the picture.)
   You're going to write about this picture.

2. The picture shows what a dog and a cat did.
   • What did the dog do? (Call on a child. Idea: *Chewed on a bone.*)
   • What did the cat do? (Call on a child. Idea: *Climbed a tree.*)

3. Listen: The dog chewed on a bone. The cat climbed a tree.
   • Everybody, say the whole sentence about the dog. (Signal.) *The dog chewed on a bone.*
   • Say the whole sentence about the cat. (Signal.) *The cat climbed a tree.* (Repeat sentences until firm.)

4. Look at the vocabulary box. These are some of the words you need: climbed . . . chewed . . . bone.

5. Say the sentence about the dog. (Signal.) *The dog chewed on a bone.*
   • Say the sentence about the cat. (Signal.) *The cat climbed a tree.*
   • Write both sentences. (Observe children and give feedback.)

6. Skip a line on your paper and write both sentences again. (Observe children and give feedback.)

Materials: BLM 13. Lined paper.

Objective: Compose and write a parallel sentence pair based on a single picture.

WRITING PARALLEL SENTENCES

1. (Display or hand out BLM 13. Point to the picture.)
   You're going to write about this picture.
2. The picture shows what a girl and a boy were doing.

- What was the girl doing? (Call on a child. Idea: *Eating popcorn.*)
- Everybody, what was the boy doing? (Signal.) *Reading a book.*

3. Listen: A girl was eating popcorn. A boy was reading a book.

- Say the whole sentence about a girl. (Signal.) *A girl was eating popcorn.*
- Say the whole sentence about a boy. (Signal.) *A boy was reading a book.* (Repeat sentences until firm.)

4. Look at the vocabulary box. These are some of the words you need: popcorn . . . reading . . . eating.

5. Say the sentence about a girl. (Signal.) *A girl was eating popcorn.*

- Say the sentence about a boy. (Signal.) *A boy was reading a book.*
- Write both sentences. (Observe children and give feedback.)

6. Skip a line on your paper and write both sentences again. (Observe children and give feedback.)

Extension Lesson 14

Materials:	BLM 14. Lined paper.
Objective:	Compose and write a parallel sentence pair based on a single picture.

WRITING PARALLEL SENTENCES

next   box   chair

BLM 14

Copyright © by SRA/McGraw-Hill. Permission is granted to reproduce this page for classroom use.

1. (Display or hand out BLM 14. Point to the picture.)
   You're going to write about this picture.
2. The picture shows what a dog and a cat sat next to.

- Where did the dog sit? (Call on a child. Idea: *Next to a chair.*)
- Where did the cat sit? (Call on a child. Idea: *Next to a box.*)
3. Listen: A dog sat next to a chair. A cat sat next to a box.
- Everybody, say the whole sentence about a dog. (Signal.) *A dog sat next to a chair.*
- Say the whole sentence about a cat. (Signal.) *A cat sat next to a box.* (Repeat sentences until firm.)
4. Look at the vocabulary box. These are some of the words you need: next . . . box . . . chair.
5. Say the sentence about a dog. (Signal.) *A dog sat next to a chair.*
- Say the sentence about a cat. (Signal.) *A cat sat next to a box.*
- Write both sentences. (Observe children and give feedback.)
6. Skip a line on your paper and write both sentences again. (Observe children and give feedback.)

Materials: BLM 15. Lined paper.

Objective: Compose and write a parallel sentence pair based on a single picture.

WRITING PARALLEL SENTENCES

BLM 15

sawed   painted   woman   board

Copyright © by SRA/McGraw-Hill. Permission is granted to reproduce this page for classroom use.

1. (Display or hand out BLM 15. Point to the picture.)
   You're going to write about this picture.
2. The picture shows what a woman and a girl did.

• What did the woman do? (Call on a child. Idea: *Painted a wall.*)
• What did the girl do? (Call on a child. Idea: *Sawed a board.*)
3. Listen: The woman painted a wall. The girl sawed a board.
• Everybody, say the whole sentence about the woman. (Signal.) *The woman painted a wall.*
• Say the whole sentence about the girl. (Signal.) *The girl sawed a board.* (Repeat sentences until firm.)
4. Look at the vocabulary box. These are some of the words you need: sawed . . . painted . . . woman . . . board.
5. Say the sentence about the woman. (Signal.) *The woman painted a wall.*
• Say the sentence about the girl. (Signal.) *The girl sawed a board.*
• Write both sentences. (Observe children and give feedback.)
6. Skip a line on your paper and write both sentences again. (Observe children and give feedback.)

Extension Lesson 16

Materials: BLM 16. Lined paper.
Objective: Compose and write a parallel sentence pair based on a single picture.

WRITING PARALLEL SENTENCES

BLM 16

skipped catch played rope

Copyright © by SRA/McGraw-Hill. Permission is granted to reproduce this page for classroom use.

1. (Display or hand out BLM 16. Point to the picture.)
   You're going to write about this picture.
2. The picture shows what boys and girls did.

- What did the boys do? (Call on a child. Idea: *Played catch.*)
- What did the girls do? (Call on a child. Idea: *Skipped rope.*)
3. Listen: The boys played catch. The girls skipped rope.
- Everybody, say the whole sentence about the boys. (Signal.) *The boys played catch.*
- Say the whole sentence about the girls. (Signal.) *The girls skipped rope.* (Repeat sentences until firm.)
4. Look at the vocabulary box. These are some of the words you need: skipped . . . catch . . . played . . . rope.
5. Say the sentence about the boys. (Signal.) *The boys played catch.*
- Say the sentence about the girls. (Signal.) *The girls skipped rope.*
- Write both sentences. (Observe children and give feedback.)
6. Skip a line on your paper and write both sentences again. (Observe children and give feedback.)

Materials: BLM 17. Lined paper.

Objective: Compose and write a parallel sentence pair based on a single picture.

WRITING PARALLEL SENTENCES

1. (Display or hand out BLM 17. Point to the picture.)
   You're going to write about this picture.
2. The picture shows what a woman and a man were doing.

- What was the woman doing? (Call on a child. Idea: *Painting a chair.*)
- What was the man doing? (Call on a child. Idea: *Sitting in a chair.*)
3. Listen: The woman was painting a chair. The man was sitting in a chair.
- Everybody, say the whole sentence about the woman. (Signal.) *The woman was painting a chair.*
- Say the whole sentence about the man. (Signal.) *The man was sitting in a chair.* (Repeat sentences until firm.)
4. Look at the vocabulary box. These are some of the words you need: chair . . . woman . . . sitting . . . painting.
5. Say the sentence about the woman. (Signal.) *The woman was painting a chair.*
- Say the sentence about the man. (Signal.) *The man was sitting in a chair.*
- Write both sentences. (Observe children and give feedback.)
6. Skip a line on your paper and write both sentences again. (Observe children and give feedback.)

Extension Lesson 18

> **Materials:** BLM 18. Lined paper.
>
> **Objective:** Compose and write a parallel sentence pair based on a single picture.

WRITING PARALLEL SENTENCES

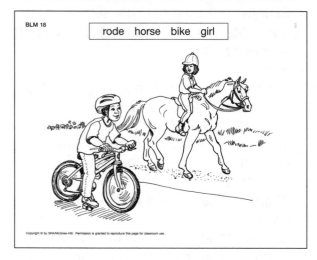

1. (Display or hand out BLM 18. Point to the picture.)
   You're going to write about this picture.
2. The picture shows what a boy and a girl did.

- What did the boy do? (Call on a child. Idea: *Rode a bike.*)
- What did the girl do? (Call on a child. Idea: *Rode a horse.*)
3. Listen: The boy rode a bike. The girl rode a horse.
- Say the whole sentence about the boy. (Signal.) *The boy rode a bike.*
- Say the whole sentence about the girl. (Signal.) *The girl rode a horse.* (Repeat sentences until firm.)
4. Look at the vocabulary box. These are some of the words you need: rode . . . horse . . . bike . . . girl.
5. Say the sentence about the boy. (Signal.) The boy rode a bike.
- Say the sentence about the girl. (Signal.) The girl rode a horse.
- Write both sentences. (Observe children and give feedback.)
6. Skip a line on your paper and write both sentences again. (Observe children and give feedback.)

| Materials: | BLM 19. Lined paper. |
| Objective: | Compose and write a parallel sentence pair based on a single picture. |

WRITING PARALLEL SENTENCES

BLM 19

mopped   washed   dishes   floor

Copyright © by SRA/McGraw-Hill. Permission is granted to reproduce this page for classroom use.

1. (Display or hand out BLM 19. Point to the picture.)
   You're going to write about this picture.
2. The picture shows what a woman and a man did.

- What did the woman do? (Call on a child. Idea: *Washed dishes.*)
- What did the man do? (Call on a child. Idea: *Mopped the floor.*)
3. Listen: The woman washed dishes. The man mopped the floor.
- Everybody, say the whole sentence about the woman. (Signal.) *The woman washed dishes.*
- Say the whole sentence about the man. (Signal.) *The man mopped the floor.* (Repeat sentences until firm.)
4. Look at the vocabulary box. These are some of the words you need: mopped . . . washed . . . dishes . . . floor.
5. Say the sentence about the woman. (Signal.) *The woman washed dishes.*
- Say the sentence about the man. (Signal.) *The man mopped the floor.*
- Write both sentences. (Observe children and give feedback.)
6. Skip a line on your paper and write both sentences again. (Observe children and give feedback.)

Extension Lesson 20

Materials: BLM 20. Lined paper.

Objective: Compose and write a parallel sentence pair based on a single picture.

WRITING PARALLEL SENTENCES

1. (Display or hand out BLM 20. Point to the picture.)
   You're going to write about this picture.
2. The picture shows what a black dog and a gray dog did.
   • What did the black dog do? (Call on a child. Idea: *Chased the rabbit.*)
   • What did the gray dog do? (Call on a child. Idea: *Scratched its ear.*)

3. Listen: The black dog chased a rabbit. The gray dog scratched its ear.
   • Everybody, say the whole sentence about the black dog. (Signal.) *The black dog chased a rabbit.*
   • Say the whole sentence about the gray dog. (Signal.) *The gray dog scratched its ear.*
   (Repeat sentences until firm.)
4. Look at the vocabulary box. These are some of the words you need: its . . . gray . . . scratched . . . chased . . . rabbit . . . ear.
5. Say the sentence about the black dog. (Signal.) *The black dog chased a rabbit.*
   • Say the sentence about the gray dog. (Signal.) *The gray dog scratched its ear.*
   • Write both sentences.
   (Observe children and give feedback.)
6. Skip a line on your paper and write both sentences again.
   (Observe children and give feedback.)

Materials: BLM 21. Lined paper.

Objective: Compose and write a parallel sentence pair based on a single picture.

WRITING PARALLEL SENTENCES

1. (Display or hand out BLM 21. Point to the picture.)
   You're going to write about this picture.
2. The picture shows what a tall woman and a short woman were doing.
   - What was the tall woman doing? (Call on a child. Idea: *Painting the ceiling.*)
   - What was the short woman doing? (Call on a child. Idea: *Painting the wall.*)

3. Listen: The tall woman was painting the ceiling. The short woman was painting the wall.
   - Say the whole sentence about the tall woman. (Signal.) *The tall woman was painting the ceiling.*
   - Say the whole sentence about the short woman. (Signal.) *The short woman was painting the wall.*
   (Repeat sentences until firm.)
4. Look at the vocabulary box. These are some of the words you need: ceiling . . . short . . . tall . . . painting.
5. Say the sentence about the tall woman. (Signal.) *The tall woman was painting the ceiling.*
   - Say the sentence about the short woman. (Signal.) *The short woman was painting the wall.*
   - Write both sentences.
   (Observe children and give feedback.)
6. Skip a line on your paper and write both sentences again.
   (Observe children and give feedback.)

Extension Lesson 22

Materials:	BLM 22. Lined paper.
Objective:	Compose and write a parallel sentence pair based on a single picture.

WRITING PARALLEL SENTENCES

1. (Display or hand out BLM 22. Point to the picture.)
   You're going to write about this picture.
2. The picture shows what a white goat and a spotted goat ate.

- What did the white goat eat? (Signal.) *Grass.*
- What did the spotted goat eat? (Call on a child. *Idea: Corn.*)
3. Listen: A white goat ate grass.
- Everybody, say the whole sentence about a white goat. (Signal.) *A white goat ate grass.*
   (Repeat the sentence until firm.)
4. Look at the vocabulary box. These are some of the words you need: ate . . . spotted . . . corn . . . white . . . goat . . . grass.
5. Write both sentences.
   (Observe children and give feedback.)
6. Check your sentences. (Call on several children to read both sentences. Idea: *A white goat ate grass. A spotted goat ate corn.*)
- Raise your hand if you got both of them right. ✔
7. Skip a line on your paper and write both sentences again.
   (Observe children and give feedback.)

Materials: BLM 23. Lined paper.

Objective: Compose and write a parallel sentence pair based on a single picture.

WRITING PARALLEL SENTENCES

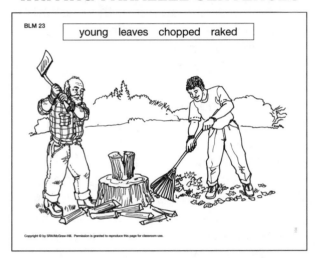

BLM 23

| young | leaves | chopped | raked |

Copyright © by SRA/McGraw-Hill. Permission is granted to reproduce this page for classroom use.

1. (Display or hand out BLM 23. Point to the picture.)
   You're going to write about this picture.
2. The picture shows what an old man and a young man did.

- What did the old man do? (Call on a child. Idea: *Chopped wood.*)
- What did the young man do? (Call on a child. Idea: *Raked leaves.*)
3. Listen: An old man chopped wood.
- Everybody, say the whole sentence about an old man. (Signal.) *An old man chopped wood.*
   (Repeat the sentence until firm.)
4. Look at the vocabulary box. These are some of the words you need: young . . . leaves . . . chopped . . . raked.
5. Write both sentences.
   (Observe children and give feedback.)
6. Check your sentences. (Call on several children to read both sentences. Idea: *An old man chopped wood. A young man raked leaves.*)
- Raise your hand if you got both of them right. ✔
7. Skip a line on your paper and write both sentences again.
   (Observe children and give feedback.)

Extension Lesson 24

> **Materials:** BLM 24. Lined paper.
>
> **Objective:** Compose and write a parallel sentence pair based on a single picture.

WRITING PARALLEL SENTENCES

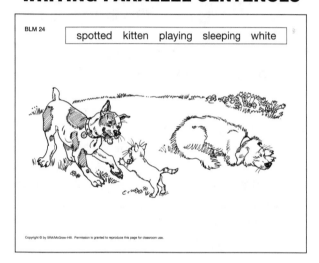

1. (Display or hand out BLM 24. Point to the picture.)
   You're going to write about this picture.
2. The picture shows what a spotted dog and a white dog were doing.

- What was the spotted dog doing? (Call on a child. Idea: *Playing with a kitten.*)
- Everybody, what was the white dog doing? (Signal.) *Sleeping.*
3. Listen: The spotted dog was playing with a kitten.
- Say the sentence about the spotted dog. (Signal.) *The spotted dog was playing with a kitten.*
  (Repeat the sentence until firm.)
4. Look at the vocabulary box. These are some of the words you need: spotted . . . kitten . . . playing . . . sleeping . . . white.
5. Write both sentences.
   (Observe children and give feedback.)
6. Check your sentences. (Call on several children to read both sentences. Idea: *The spotted dog was playing with a kitten. The white dog was sleeping.*)
- Raise your hand if you got both of them right. ✔
7. Skip a line on your paper and write both sentences again.
   (Observe children and give feedback.)

Materials: BLM 25. Lined paper.

Objective: Compose and write a parallel sentence pair based on a single picture.

WRITING PARALLEL SENTENCES

1. (Display or hand out BLM 25. Point to the picture.)
   You're going to write about this picture.
2. The picture shows what an old woman and a young woman were carrying.
   - What was the old woman carrying? (Call on a child. Idea: *A box.*)
   - Everybody, what was the young woman carrying? (Signal.) *A bike.*

3. Listen: An old woman was carrying a box.
   - Say the sentence about an old woman. (Signal.) *An old woman was carrying a box.*
     (Repeat the sentence until firm.)
4. Look at the vocabulary box. These are words you need: were . . . carrying . . . box . . . woman . . . young . . . bike.
5. Write both sentences.
   (Observe children and give feedback.)
6. Check your sentences. (Call on several children to read both sentences. Idea: *An old woman was carrying a box. A young woman was carrying a bike.*)
   - Raise your hand if you got both of them right. ✔
7. Skip a line on your paper and write both sentences again.
   (Observe children and give feedback.)

Extension Lesson 26

Materials: BLM 26. Lined paper.

Objective: Compose and write a parallel sentence pair based on a single picture.

WRITING PARALLEL SENTENCES

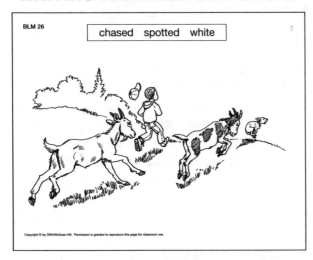

1. (Display or hand out BLM 26. Point to the picture.)

   You're going to write about this picture.

2. The picture shows what a white goat and a spotted goat chased.

- What did the white goat chase? (Call on a child. Idea: *A boy.*)
- Everybody, what did the spotted goat chase? (Signal.) *A dog.*

3. Listen: A white goat chased a boy.

- Say the sentence about a white goat. (Signal.) *A white goat chased a boy.* (Repeat the sentence until firm.)

4. Look at the vocabulary box. These are words you need: chased . . . spotted . . . white.

5. Write both sentences. (Observe children and give feedback.)

6. Check your sentences. (Call on several children to read both sentences. Idea: *A white goat chased a boy. A spotted goat chased a dog.*)

- Raise your hand if you got both of them right. ✔

7. Skip a line on your paper and write both sentences again. (Observe children and give feedback.)

Materials: BLM 27. Lined paper.

Objective: Compose and write a parallel sentence pair based on a single picture.

WRITING PARALLEL SENTENCES

1. (Display or hand out BLM 27. Point to the picture.)

   You're going to write about this picture.
2. The picture shows what an older boy and a younger boy were doing.

- What was the older boy doing? (Call on a child. Idea: *Rowing a boat.*)
- Everybody, what was the younger boy doing? (Signal.) *Fishing.*
3. Listen: An older boy was rowing a boat.
- Say the sentence about an older boy. (Signal.) *An older boy was rowing a boat.*
   (Repeat the sentence until firm.)
4. Look at the vocabulary box. These are words you need: younger . . . boat . . . fishing . . . rowing.
5. Write both sentences.
   (Observe children and give feedback.)
6. Check your sentences. (Call on several children to read both sentences. Idea: *An older boy was rowing a boat. A younger boy was fishing.*)
- Raise your hand if you got both of them right. ✔
7. Skip a line on your paper and write both sentences again.
   (Observe children and give feedback.)

Extension Lesson 28

Materials: BLM 28. Lined paper.

Objective: Compose and write a parallel sentence pair based on a single picture.

WRITING PARALLEL SENTENCES

1. (Display or hand out BLM 28. Point to the picture.)
   You're going to write about this picture.
2. The picture shows what a younger girl and an older girl were doing.

- What was the younger girl doing? (Call on a child. Idea: *Drawing.*)
- What was the older girl doing? (Call on a child. Idea: *Skipping rope.*)
3. Listen: The younger girl was drawing.
- Say the sentence about the younger girl. (Signal.) *The younger girl was drawing.*
  (Repeat the sentence until firm.)
4. Look at the vocabulary box. These are words you need: drawing . . . skipping . . . younger . . . older . . . girl.
5. Write both sentences.
   (Observe children and give feedback.)
6. Check your sentences. (Call on several children to read both sentences. Idea: *The younger girl was drawing. The older girl was skipping rope.*)
- Raise your hand if you got both of them right. ✔
7. Skip a line on your paper and write both sentences again.
   (Observe children and give feedback.)

Materials: BLM 29. Lined paper.

Objective: Compose and write a parallel sentence pair based on a single picture.

WRITING PARALLEL SENTENCES

1. (Display or hand out BLM 29. Point to the picture.)
   You're going to write about this picture.
2. The picture shows what two girls and two boys were doing.

- What were the girls doing? (Call on a child. Idea: *Eating ice cream.*)
- Everybody, what were the boys doing? (Signal.) *Swimming.*
3. Listen: The girls were eating ice cream.
- Say the sentence about the girls. (Signal.) *The girls were eating ice cream.*
   (Repeat the sentence until firm.)
4. Look at the vocabulary box. These are words you need: swimming . . . eating . . . were . . . ice cream.
5. Write both sentences.
   (Observe children and give feedback.)
6. Check your sentences. (Call on several children to read both sentences. Idea: *The girls were eating ice cream. The boys were swimming.*)
- Raise your hand if you got both of them right. ✔
7. Skip a line on your paper and write both sentences again.
   (Observe children and give feedback.)

Extension Lesson 30

Materials: BLM 30. Lined paper.

Objective: Compose and write a parallel sentence pair based on a single picture.

WRITING PARALLEL SENTENCES

1. (Display or hand out BLM 30. Point to the picture.)
   You're going to write about this picture.
2. The picture shows what two men and two women were doing.

- What were the men doing? (Call on a child. Idea: *Sleeping.*)
- Everybody, what were the women doing? (Signal.) *Reading.*
3. Listen: The women were reading.
- Say the sentence about the women. (Signal.) *The women were reading.* (Repeat the sentence until firm.)
4. Look at the vocabulary box. These are words you need: sleeping . . . reading . . . women . . . were.
5. Write both sentences.
   (Observe children and give feedback.)
6. Check your sentences. (Call on several children to read both sentences. Idea: *The women were reading. The men were sleeping.*)
- Raise your hand if you got both of them right. ✔
7. Skip a line on your paper and write both sentences again.
   (Observe children and give feedback.)

Extension Lesson 31

Materials:	BLM 31. Lined paper.
Objective:	Compose and write a parallel sentence pair based on a single picture.

WRITING PARALLEL SENTENCES

BLM 31

horses   running   goats   eating

Copyright © by SRA/McGraw-Hill. Permission is granted to reproduce this page for classroom use.

1. (Display or hand out BLM 31. Point to the picture.)
   You're going to write about this picture.
2. The picture shows what two horses and two goats were doing.

- What were the horses doing? (Signal.) *Eating.*
- What were the goats doing? (Call on a child. Idea: *Running.*)

3. Listen: The horses were eating.

- Everybody, say the sentence about the horses. (Signal.) *The horses were eating.*
  (Repeat the sentence until firm.)

4. Look at the vocabulary box. These are words you need: horses . . . running . . . goats . . . eating.
5. Write both sentences.
   (Observe children and give feedback.)
6. Check your sentences. (Call on several children to read both sentences. Idea: *The horses were eating. The goats were running.*)

- Raise your hand if you got both of them right. ✔

7. Skip a line on your paper and write both sentences again.
   (Observe children and give feedback.)

Extension Lesson 32

Materials: BLM 32. Lined paper.

Objective: Compose and write a parallel sentence pair based on a single picture.

WRITING PARALLEL SENTENCES

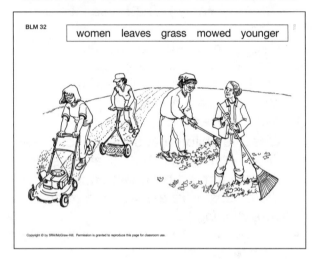

BLM 32

| women | leaves | grass | mowed | younger |

Copyright © by SRA/McGraw-Hill. Permission is granted to reproduce this page for classroom use.

1. (Display or hand out BLM 32. Point to the picture.)
   You're going to write about this picture.
2. The picture shows what two older women and two younger women did.

- What did the older women do? (Call on a child. Idea: *Raked leaves.*)
- What did the younger women do? (Call on a child. Idea: *Mowed the grass.*)
3. Listen: The older women raked leaves.
- Everybody, say the sentence about the older women. (Signal.) *The older women raked leaves.*
  (Repeat the sentence until firm.)
4. Look at the vocabulary box. These are words you need: women . . . leaves . . . grass . . . mowed . . . younger.
5. Write both sentences.
   (Observe children and give feedback.)
6. Check your sentences. (Call on several children to read both sentences. Idea: *The older women raked leaves. The younger women mowed the grass.*)
- Raise your hand if you got both of them right. ✔
7. Skip a line on your paper and write both sentences again.
   (Observe children and give feedback.)

Extension Lesson 33

Materials: BLM 33. Lined paper.

Objective: Compose and write a parallel sentence pair based on a single picture.

WRITING PARALLEL SENTENCES

1. (Display or hand out BLM 33. Point to the picture.)
   You're going to write about this picture.
2. The picture shows what two younger men and two older men did.

- What did the younger men do? (Call on a child. Idea: *Set the table.*)
- What did the older men do? (Call on a child. Idea: *Washed the dishes.*)
3. Listen: The younger men set the table.
- Everybody, say the sentence about the younger men. (Signal.) *The younger men set the table.*
   (Repeat the sentence until firm.)
4. Look at the vocabulary box. These are words you need: dishes . . . younger . . . table . . . washed . . . set.
5. Write both sentences.
   (Observe children and give feedback.)
6. Check your sentences. (Call on several children to read both sentences. Idea: *The younger men set the table. The older men washed the dishes.*)
- Raise your hand if you got both of them right. ✔
7. Skip a line on your paper and write both sentences again.
   (Observe children and give feedback.)

Extension Lesson 34

> **Materials:** BLM 34. Lined paper.
> **Objective:** Compose and write a parallel sentence pair based on a single picture.

WRITING PARALLEL SENTENCES

1. (Display or hand out BLM 34. Point to the picture.)
   You're going to write about this picture.
2. The picture shows what two older girls and two younger girls were doing.

- What were the older girls doing? (Call on a child. Idea: *Watching TV*.)
- What were the younger girls doing? (Call on a child. Idea: *Reading a book.*)
3. Listen: The younger girls were reading a book.
- Everybody, say the sentence about the younger girls. (Signal.) *The younger girls were reading a book.* (Repeat the sentence until firm.)
4. Look at the vocabulary box. These are words you need: watching . . . were . . . TV.
5. Write both sentences.
   (Observe children and give feedback.)
6. Check your sentences. (Call on several children to read both sentences. Idea: *The younger girls were reading a book. The older girls were watching TV.*)
- Raise your hand if you got both of them right. ✔
7. Skip a line on your paper and write both sentences again.
   (Observe children and give feedback.)

Materials: BLM 35. Lined paper.

Objective: Compose and write a parallel sentence pair based on a single picture.

WRITING PARALLEL SENTENCES

1. (Display or hand out BLM 35. Point to the picture.)
   You're going to write about this picture.
2. The picture shows what two spotted horses and two black horses were doing.

- What were the spotted horses doing? (Signal.) *Running.*
- What were the black horses doing? (Call on a child. Idea: *Eating grass.*)
3. Listen: The black horses were eating grass.
- Everybody, say the sentence about the black horses. (Signal.) *The black horses were eating grass.*
   (Repeat the sentence until firm.)
4. Look at the vocabulary box. These are words you need: horses . . . grass . . . were . . . spotted . . . eating . . . running.
5. Write both sentences.
   (Observe children and give feedback.)
6. Check your sentences. (Call on several children to read both sentences. Idea: *The black horses were eating grass. The spotted horses were running.*)
- Raise your hand if you got both of them right. ✔
7. Skip a line on your paper and write both sentences again.
   (Observe children and give feedback.)

Extension Lesson 36

Materials: BLM 36. Lined paper.

Objective: Compose and write a parallel sentence pair based on a single picture.

WRITING PARALLEL SENTENCES

1. (Display or hand out BLM 36. Point to the picture.)
   You're going to write about this picture.
2. The picture shows what two black cats and two white cats did.

- What did the black cats do? (Call on a child. Idea: *Climbed a tree.*)
- What did the white cats do? (Call on a child. Idea: *Sat on a car.*)
3. Listen: The black cats climbed a tree.
- Everybody, say the sentence about the black cats. (Signal.) *The black cats climbed a tree.*
  (Repeat the sentence until firm.)
4. Look at the vocabulary box. This is a word you need: climbed.
5. Write both sentences.
   (Observe children and give feedback.)
6. Check your sentences. (Call on several children to read both sentences. Idea: *The black cats climbed a tree. The white cats sat on a car.*)
- Raise your hand if you got both of them right. ✔
7. Skip a line on your paper and write both sentences again.
   (Observe children and give feedback.)

Materials: BLM 37. Lined paper.

Objective: Compose and write a parallel sentence pair based on a single picture.

WRITING PARALLEL SENTENCES

1. (Display or hand out BLM 37. Point to the picture.)
   You're going to write about this picture.
2. The picture shows what two girls and two women did.

- What did the girls do? (Call on a child. Idea: *Washed the windows.*)
- Everybody, what did the women do? (Signal.) *Swept the floor.*
3. Listen: The girls washed the windows.
- Say the sentence about the girls. (Signal.) *The girls washed the windows.* (Repeat the sentence until firm.)
4. Look at the vocabulary box. These are words you need: floor . . . washed . . . swept . . . windows . . . women.
5. Write both sentences. (Observe children and give feedback.)
6. Check your sentences. (Call on several children to read both sentences. Idea: *The girls washed the windows. The women swept the floor.*)
- Raise your hand if you got both of them right. ✔
7. Skip a line on your paper and write both sentences again. (Observe children and give feedback.)

Extension Lesson 38

Materials: BLM 38. Lined paper.

Objective: Compose and write a parallel sentence pair based on a single picture.

WRITING PARALLEL SENTENCES

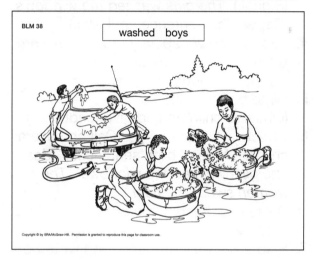

1. (Display or hand out BLM 38. Point to the picture.)
   You're going to write about this picture.
2. The picture shows what two boys and two men did.

- What did the boys do? (Call on a child. Idea: *Washed the car.*)
- What did the men do? (Call on a child. Idea: *Washed the dogs.*)

3. Listen: The men washed the dogs.
- Everybody, say the sentence about the men. (Signal.) *The men washed the dogs.*
   (Repeat the sentence until firm.)
4. Look at the vocabulary box. These are words you need: washed . . . boys.
5. Write both sentences.
   (Observe children and give feedback.)
6. Check your sentences. (Call on several children to read both sentences. Idea: *The men washed the dogs. The boys washed the car.*)
- Raise your hand if you got both of them right. ✔
7. Skip a line on your paper and write both sentences again.
   (Observe children and give feedback.)

Materials: BLM 39. Lined paper.

Objective: Compose and write a parallel sentence pair based on a single picture.

WRITING PARALLEL SENTENCES

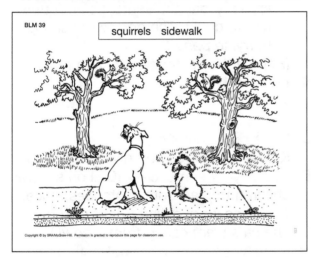

1. (Display or hand out BLM 39. Point to the picture.)

   You're going to write about this picture.

2. The picture shows where two squirrels sat and where two dogs sat.

- Where did the squirrels sit? (Call on a child. Idea: *In the trees.*)
- Everybody, where did the dogs sit? (Signal.) *On the sidewalk.*

3. Listen: The squirrels sat in the trees.

- Say the sentence about the squirrels. (Signal.) *The squirrels sat in the trees.* (Repeat the sentence until firm.)

4. Look at the vocabulary box. These are words you need: squirrels . . . sidewalk.

5. Write both sentences. (Observe children and give feedback.)

6. Check your sentences. (Call on several children to read both sentences. Idea: *The squirrels sat in the trees. The dogs sat on the sidewalk.*)

- Raise your hand if you got both of them right. ✔

7. Skip a line on your paper and write both sentences again. (Observe children and give feedback.)

Extension Lesson 40

> **Materials:** BLM 40. Lined paper.
>
> **Objective:** Compose and write a parallel sentence pair based on a single picture.

WRITING PARALLEL SENTENCES

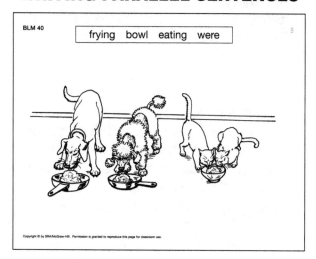

1. (Display or hand out BLM 40. Point to the picture.)
   You're going to write about this picture.
2. The picture shows what kind of containers the animals were eating from.

- What were the dogs eating from? (Call on a child. Idea: *Frying pans.*)
- What were the cats eating from? (Call on a child. Idea: *A bowl.*)
3. Listen: The dogs were eating from frying pans.
- Everybody, say the sentence about the dogs. (Signal.) *The dogs were eating from frying pans.*
   (Repeat the sentence until firm.)
4. Look at the vocabulary box. These are words you need: frying . . . bowl . . . eating . . . were.
5. Write both sentences.
   (Observe children and give feedback.)
6. Check your sentences. (Call on several children to read both sentences. Idea: *The dogs were eating from frying pans. The cats were eating from a bowl.*)
- Raise your hand if you got both of them right. ✔
7. Skip a line on your paper and write both sentences again.
   (Observe children and give feedback.)

Materials: BLM 41. Lined paper.

Objective: Compose and write a parallel sentence pair based on a single picture.

WRITING PARALLEL SENTENCES

1. (Display or hand out BLM 41. Point to the picture.)
   You're going to write about this picture.
2. The picture shows what two dogs and two rabbits ate from.

- What did the dogs do? (Call on a child. Idea: *Ate from a frying pan.*)
- What did the rabbits do? (Call on a child. Idea: *Ate from bowls.*)
3. Listen: The dogs ate from a frying pan.
- Everybody, say the sentence about the dogs. (Signal.) *The dogs ate from a frying pan.*
  (Repeat the sentence until firm.)
4. Look at the vocabulary box. These are words you need: rabbits . . . frying . . . bowls . . . ate.
5. Write both sentences.
   (Observe children and give feedback.)
6. Check your sentences. (Call on several children to read both sentences. Idea: *The dogs ate from a frying pan. The rabbits ate from bowls.*)
- Raise your hand if you got both of them right. ✔
7. Skip a line on your paper and write both sentences again.
   (Observe children and give feedback.)

Extension Lesson 42

Materials: BLM 42. Lined paper.

Objective A: Write three sentences based on a 3-picture sequence.

Objective B: Rewrite the sentences.

EXERCISE A
SEQUENCE SENTENCE WRITING

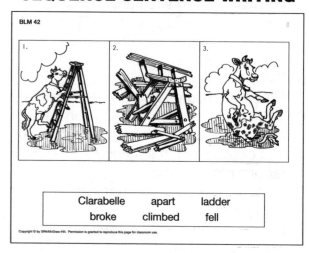

1. (Display or hand out BLM 42. Point to the pictures.)
   You're going to report on what these pictures show.
2. Picture 1. What did Clarabelle do in that picture? **(Call on a child. Idea:** *Climbed a ladder.*)
   • Picture 2. What did the ladder do? Start with the words **the ladder** and say a sentence that tells what the ladder did. **(Call on several children. Ideas:** *The ladder fell apart. The ladder broke into pieces.*)

   • Picture 3. What did Clarabelle do when the ladder broke? **(Call on several children. Ideas:** *Fell in the mud. Clarabelle fell on the ground.*)
3. Look at the vocabulary box.

Clarabelle	apart	ladder
broke	climbed	fell

   These are words you could use.
4. Write your sentence for picture 1. Start with the word **Clarabelle.** Tell what Clarabelle did in that picture. Don't tell what she was doing. Pencils down when you're finished.
   (Observe children and give feedback.)
   • Write your sentence for picture 2. Start with the words **the ladder.** Tell what it did. Pencils down when you're finished.
   (Observe children and give feedback.)
   • Write your sentence for picture 3. Start with the word **Clarabelle.** Pencils down when you're finished.
   (Observe children and give feedback.)
5. (Call on different children to read their sentences. Praise good sentences. Tell how to fix up sentences with problems.)
6. (Collect papers. Mark errors in clarity, spelling and punctuation. During the next language period, pass back the corrected papers and present Exercise B.)

EXERCISE B

REWRITING

- (Return corrected papers to children.)
You did a good job the first time you wrote about Clarabelle and the ladder. Now you're going to write a perfect paper. Rewrite the whole story from the beginning. Write it so it doesn't have any mistakes.

- (After children complete their final draft, post the papers [and the children's illustrations] of the story.)

Extension Lesson 43

EXERCISE A
SEQUENCE SENTENCE WRITING

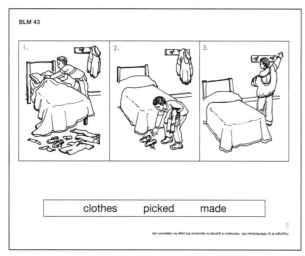

1. (Display or hand out BLM 43. Point to the pictures.)
   You're going to report on what these pictures show.
2. Picture 1. What did the boy do in that picture? (Call on a child. Idea: *Made the bed.*)
   • Picture 2. Start with the word **then** and say a sentence about picture 2. (Call on a child. Idea: *Then he picked up his clothes.*)
   • Picture 3. Start with the word **then** and tell what he did in picture 3. (Call on a child. Idea: *Then he put on his coat.*)

3. Look at the vocabulary box.

clothes	picked	made

   These are words you could use.
4. Write your sentence for picture 1. Start with the words **the boy** and tell what he did in that picture. Pencils down when you're finished.
   (Observe children and give feedback.)
   • Write your sentence for picture 2. Start with the word **then.** Tell what he did. Pencils down when you're finished.
   (Observe children and give feedback.)
   • Write your sentence for picture 3. Start with the word **then.** Pencils down when you're finished.
   (Observe children and give feedback.)
5. (Call on different children to read their sentences. Praise good sentences. Tell how to fix up sentences with problems.)
6. (Collect papers. Mark errors in clarity, spelling and punctuation. During the next language period, pass back the corrected papers and present Exercise B.)

EXERCISE B
REWRITING

• (Return corrected papers to children.)
  You did a good job the first time you wrote about the boy. Now you're going to write a perfect paper. Rewrite the whole story from the beginning. Write it so it doesn't have any mistakes.
• (After children complete their final draft, post the papers [and the children's illustrations] of the story.)

Materials: BLM 44. Lined paper.

Objective: **Write three directions telling how to make two things the same.**

WRITING DIRECTIONS
Making Two Things the Same

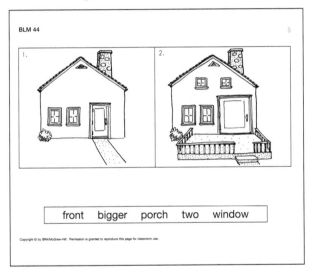

1. (Display or hand out BLM 44. Point to the pictures.)
   The pictures show two houses. They are the same in a lot of ways and different in some ways. You're going to write the things you would have to do to make house 1 look exactly like house 2. The first thing we do is name all the ways house 2 is different from house 1.

2. Name one way house 2 is different. (Call on different children.)

• (Repeat step 2 until all differences are identified. Praise good descriptions.)

Key:
  • *House 2 has a larger front door.*
  • *House 2 has four windows.*
  • *House 2 has a front porch.*

3. Listen: One of the ways the houses are different is that house 2 has a larger front door. Start with the word **make** and say a sentence that tells how you would change house 1. (Call on a child. Idea: *Make the front door bigger. Make a bigger front door on house 1.*)

• Another difference is that house 2 has four windows. Everybody, how many windows does house 1 have?
  (Signal.) *Two.*
  Start with the word **make** and say a sentence that tells how you would change house 1. (Call on a child. Idea: *Make two more windows in the front of house 1.*)

• Another difference is that house 2 has a front porch. Say a sentence that starts with the word **make** and tells how you would change house 1. (Call on a child. Idea: *Make a porch on the front of the house. Make a porch with rails and a step.*)

4. The vocabulary box shows some of the words that you may want to use when you write your directions.

front	bigger	porch	two	window

5. (Write on the board:)

How to Change House One

- Use lined paper. On the top line write this title. It tells what you'll write about. Pencils down when you've written the title.
(Observe children and give feedback.)

6. Now write three sentences that tell how you would change house 1. Start each sentence with the word **make.** Pencils down when you're finished.
(Observe children and give feedback.)

7. (Call on different children to read their sentences. Praise good sentences. Tell how to correct sentences that are inadequate.)

Materials: BLM 45. Lined paper.

Objective: Write three directions telling how to make two things the same.

WRITING DIRECTIONS
Making Two Things the Same

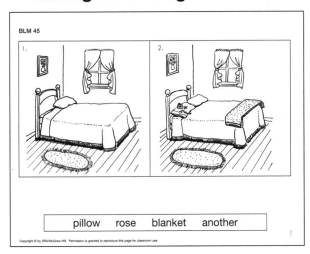

1. (Display or hand out BLM 45. Point to the pictures.)
   The pictures show two beds. They are the same in a lot of ways and different in some ways. You're going to write the things you would have to do to make bed 1 look exactly like bed 2.
   The first thing we do is name all the ways bed 2 is different from bed 1.

2. Name one way bed 2 is different. (Call on different children.)

 • (Repeat step 2 until all differences are identified. Praise good descriptions.)

Key:
 • *Bed 2 has two pillows.*
 • *Bed 2 has another blanket.*
 • *Bed 2 has a rose on the left pillow.*

3. Listen: One of the ways the beds are different is that bed 2 has two pillows. Start with the word **put** and say a sentence that tells what you would put on bed 1. (Call on a child. Idea: *Put another pillow on bed 1.*)

 • Another difference is that bed 2 has more blankets than bed 1. Start with the word **put** and say a sentence that tells what you would put at the foot of bed 1. (Call on a child. Idea: *Put a blanket at the foot of bed 1.*)

 • Start with the word **put** and say a sentence that tells the last thing you would do to make bed 2 look like bed 1. Remember, you have to tell if the rose goes on the left pillow or the right pillow. (Call on a child. Idea: *Put a rose on the left pillow.*)

4. The vocabulary box shows some of the words that you may want to use when you write your directions.

pillow	rose	blanket	another

5. (Write on the board:)

How to Change Bed One

- Use lined paper. On the top line write this title. It tells what you'll write about. Pencils down when you've written the title.
(Observe children and give feedback.)

6. Now write three sentences that tell how you would change bed 1. Start each sentence with the word **put.** Pencils down when you're finished.
(Observe children and give feedback.)

7. (Call on different children to read their sentences. Praise good sentences. Tell how to correct sentences that are inadequate.)

Materials: BLM 46. Lined paper.

Objective: Write three directions telling how to make two things the same.

WRITING DIRECTIONS
Making Two Things the Same

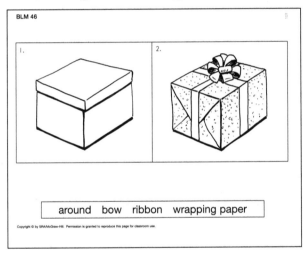

1. (Display or hand out BLM 46. Point to the pictures.)
   You're going to write the things you would have to do to make box 1 look exactly like box 2.
2. Name one way box 2 is different from box 1. **(Call on different children.)**
   - (Repeat step 2 until all differences are identified. Praise good descriptions.)
   Key:
   - *Box 2 has wrapping paper.*
   - *Box 2 has ribbon around it.*
   - *Box 2 has a bow on top.*

3. Listen: One of the ways the boxes are different is that box 2 has wrapping paper on it. Start with the word **put** and say a sentence that tells where you would put wrapping paper. **(Call on a child. Idea:** *Put wrapping paper on box 1.***)**
   - Another difference is that box 2 has ribbon around it. Start with the word **put** and say a sentence that tells where you would put the ribbon. **(Call on a child. Idea:** *Put a ribbon around box 1.***)**
   - Another difference is that box 2 has a bow on it. Say a sentence that starts with the word **put** and tells about the bow. **(Call on a child. Idea:** *Put a bow on top of the box.***)**
4. The vocabulary box shows some of the words that you may want to use when you write your directions.

around	bow	ribbon	wrapping paper

5. (Write on the board:)

   ### How to Change Box One

   - Use lined paper. On the top line write this title. It tells what you'll write about. Pencils down when you've written the title.
   (Observe children and give feedback.)

46

6. Now write three sentences that tell how you would change box 1. Start each sentence with the word **put.** Pencils down when you're finished.
(Observe children and give feedback.)

7. (Call on different children to read their sentences. Praise good sentences. Tell how to correct sentences that are inadequate.)

Materials: BLM 47. Lined paper.
Objective: **Copy a paragraph.**

BLM   **Lined Paper**

PARAGRAPH COPYING

1. (Display or hand out BLM 47.)
   You're going to copy a paragraph. A paragraph is a group of sentences that tells about the same topic or idea. The paragraph you're going to copy tells what happened to a bird that fell out of a tree.

2. When you write a paragraph, you have to think about the margin of your paper. Remember, the margin is the up-and-down line. What is the up-and-down line? (Signal.) *The margin.*

• Run your finger up and down the margin of your lined paper. ✔

3. Listen: The first line of a paragraph does not begin at the margin. Say that. (Signal.) *The first line of a paragraph does not begin at the margin.* All the other lines of the paragraph begin at the margin.

• Listen: You must indent the first line. You indent by writing the first word two fingers from the margin. The picture shows you where to put your fingers.

• (Point to the first word on BLM 47.) This is the first word in the paragraph. Everybody, is the first word of the paragraph written next to the margin? (Signal.) *No.*

• The first word of a paragraph starts two fingers from the margin. Say that. (Signal.) *The first word of a paragraph starts two fingers from the margin.*

• (Point to the second line.) Look at the second line in the paragraph. It starts right after the margin. Remember, you indent only the first line. The other lines start at the margin.

4. Look at your lined paper. You're going to start your paragraph on the first line. Put two fingers next to the margin on your paper, just like the two fingers in the picture. Don't draw your fingers. You make a capital **A** right after your fingers.

(Observe children and give feedback.)

5. You wrote the first word of the paragraph. Now copy the rest of the first sentence. Then stop. Be sure to end the sentence with a period. Pencils down when you've finished the first sentence.
(Observe children and give feedback.)

6. Touch the period at the end of the first sentence you wrote. ✔

• That's where you'll start writing the next sentence. Make a capital I just after the period. Then copy the rest of the paragraph. Remember to start each new sentence just after the period. And don't indent any more lines. Start them at the margin. You have 3 minutes. Pencils down when you're finished.
(Observe children and give feedback.)

7. (After 3 minutes, say:) Everybody, stop. Raise your hand if you're finished. **(Praise children who finished.)**

• Remember, a paragraph is a group of sentences that tells about the same topic or idea. You indent the first line of the paragraph. All the other lines of the paragraph start at the margin.

Materials: BLM 48. Lined paper.

Objective: **Write a paragraph based on a familiar picture.**

PARAGRAPH WRITING

1. (Display or hand out BLM 48. Point to the picture.)
   You've written sentences about this picture before. This time, you're going to write a whole paragraph about this picture.
2. You'll start with a sentence that tells what the group of women were doing. Listen: Were the women painting a car?
   (Signal.) *No.*
   Were the women building a boat?
   (Signal.) *No.*

- Start with the words **the women** and say a sentence that tells what the women were doing in the picture. (Call on different children. Ideas: *The women were working in the yard. The women were making the yard look good.*)
  Yes, a good first sentence would tell that the women were working in the yard or the women were making the yard look good.
- Write your first sentence of the paragraph. Start at the top line. Indent the first line. Put two fingers next to the margin and start writing after the fingers. Pencils down when you've written your first sentence. Remember to use words in the vocabulary box if you need them.
  (Observe children and give feedback.)
3. You told about what all the women were doing. Now you'll write a sentence that tells about the older women and write another sentence that tells about the younger women. Remember, all your sentences will tell what they were doing.
- Your turn: Write sentences about the older women and the younger women. Pencils down when you're finished.
  (Observe children and give feedback.)
4. (Call on different children to read their paragraphs. Praise paragraphs that have a good opening sentence and good sentences for the older and younger women.)

Extension Lesson 49

Materials: BLM 49. Lined paper.

Objective: Write a paragraph based on a familiar picture.

PARAGRAPH WRITING

BLM 49

| are | everybody | something | washing | is |

1. (Display or hand out BLM 49. Point to the picture.)
   You've written sentences about this picture before. This time, you're going to write a whole paragraph about this picture.
2. You'll start with a sentence that tells what everybody was doing. Listen: Was everybody painting a car? (Signal.) *No.*

- Start with the words **everybody was** and tell what everybody was doing in the picture. (Call on different children. Ideas: *Everybody was washing. Everybody was washing something. Everybody was using soap and water.*) Yes, a good first sentence would tell that everybody was washing something or everybody was using soap and water.
- Write your first sentence of the paragraph. Start at the top line. Indent the first line. Put two fingers next to the margin and start writing after the fingers. Pencils down when you've written your first sentence. Remember to use words in the vocabulary box if you need them. (Observe children and give feedback.)
3. You told about what everybody was doing. Now you'll write a sentence that tells about the boys and another sentence that tells about the men. Remember, all your sentences will tell what they were doing.
- Your turn: Write sentences about the boys and the men. Pencils down when you're finished. (Observe children and give feedback.)
4. (Call on different children to read their paragraphs. Praise paragraphs that have a good opening sentence and good sentences for the boys and men.)

Extension Lesson 50

Materials: BLM 50. Lined paper.

Objective: Write a paragraph based on a familiar picture.

PARAGRAPH WRITING

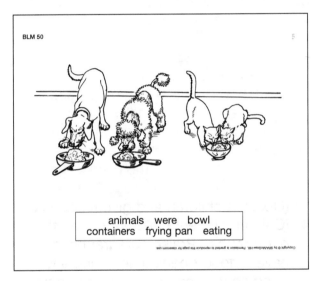

1. (Display or hand out BLM 50. Point to the picture.)
   You've written sentences about this picture before. This time, you're going to write a whole paragraph about this picture.
2. You'll start with a sentence that tells what all the animals were doing. Listen: Were the animals sleeping? **(Signal.)** *No.*

- Start with the words **the animals were** and tell what the animals were doing in the picture. **(Call on different children. Ideas:** *The animals were eating. The animals were eating from containers.***)** Yes, a good first sentence would tell that the animals were eating or the animals were eating from containers.
- Write your first sentence of the paragraph. Remember to indent the first line of your paragraph. Pencils down when you've written your first sentence. Remember to use words in the vocabulary box if you need them. **(Observe children and give feedback.)**
3. You told the main thing that all the animals were doing. Now you'll write a sentence that tells about the dogs and another sentence that tells about the cats. Remember, all your sentences will tell what they were doing, not what they are doing.
- Your turn: Write sentences about the dogs and the cats. Pencils down when you're finished. **(Observe children and give feedback.)**
4. (Call on different children to read their paragraphs. Praise paragraphs that have a good opening sentence and good sentences for the dogs and cats.)

Extension Lesson 51

Materials: BLM 51. Lined paper.

Objective: Write a paragraph based on a familiar picture.

PARAGRAPH WRITING

1. (Display or hand out BLM 51. Point to the picture.)
   You've written sentences about this picture before. This time, you're going to write a whole paragraph about this picture.

2. You'll start with a sentence that tells where the horses were. Listen: Were the horses in a barn? **(Signal.)** *No.*

   • Start with the words **the horses** and tell where the horses were in the picture. **(Call on different children. Ideas:** *The horses were in a field. The horses were outdoors.***)**
   Yes, a good first sentence would tell that the horses were in a field or the horses were outdoors.

   • Write your first sentence of the paragraph. Remember to indent. Pencils down when you've written your first sentence. Use words in the vocabulary box if you need them. **(Observe children and give feedback.)**

3. You told where the animals were. Now you'll write sentences that tell what the animals did. You'll write a sentence that tells what the spotted horses did and another sentence that tells what the black horses did. Remember, both those sentences will tell what the horses did, not what they are doing.

   • Your turn: Write sentences about the spotted horses and the black horses. Pencils down when you're finished. **(Observe children and give feedback.)**

4. **(Call on different children to read their paragraphs. Praise paragraphs that have a good opening sentence and good sentences for the spotted horses and black horses.)**

Materials: BLM 52. Lined paper.

Objective: Write a paragraph based on a familiar picture.

PARAGRAPH WRITING

1. (Display or hand out BLM 52. Point to the picture.)
You've written sentences about this picture before. This time, you're going to write a whole paragraph about this picture.

2. You'll start with a sentence that tells what the women did. Did each woman sit on something? **(Signal.)** *No.*

- Start with the words **each woman** and tell what each woman did. **(Call on a child. Idea:** *Each woman carried something.***)**
Yes, a good first sentence would tell that each woman carried something.

- Write your first sentence of the paragraph. Remember to indent. Pencils down when you've written your first sentence. Use words in the vocabulary box if you need them. **(Observe children and give feedback.)**

3. Now you'll write sentences that tell the thing that each woman carried. You'll write a sentence that tells what the older woman carried and a sentence that tells what the younger woman carried. Remember, both those sentences will tell what each woman did, not what she was doing.

- Your turn: Write sentences about what each woman carried. Pencils down when you're finished.
(Observe children and give feedback.)

4. (Call on different children to read their paragraphs. Praise paragraphs that have a good opening sentence and good sentences for the older woman and the younger woman. Correct sentences that have problems.)

Extension Lesson 53

Materials: BLM 53. Lined paper.

Objective A: **Write a paragraph based on four pictures.**

Objective B: **Rewrite the paragraph.**

EXERCISE A
PARAGRAPH WRITING

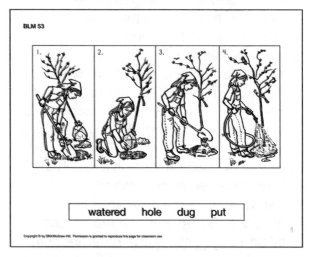

1. (Display or hand out BLM 53. Point to the pictures.)
   You're going to write a paragraph about what these pictures show.
2. You'll start with a good first sentence. A good first sentence would tell what the girl did in these pictures.
   Everybody, did the girl fix a car?
   (Signal.) *No.*
   • What did the girl do in these pictures? **(Call on a child. Idea:** *Planted a tree.***)**
   Yes, the girl planted a tree.

• Write a good first sentence that tells about what the girl did. Remember to indent the first line of the paragraph. Pencils down when you're finished. **(Observe children and give feedback.)**
• (Call on different children to read their first sentence.)
3. (Write on the board:)

> **First**
>
> **Then**

Now you're going to tell how the girl did that. The words on the board show the first word of each sentence. The sentence for picture 1 begins with the word **first.** The sentences for the next pictures start with the word **then.**

4. Picture 1. What did the girl do in that picture? **(Call on a child. Idea:** *Dug a hole.***)**
• Start with the words **first she** and say a good sentence for the first picture. **(Call on a child. Idea:** *First she dug a hole.***)**
• Picture 2. Start with the words **then she** and say a sentence about picture 2. **(Call on a child. Idea:** *Then she put the tree in the hole.***)**
• Picture 3. Start with the word **then** and tell what she did in picture 3. **(Call on a child. Idea:** *Then she put dirt in the hole.***)**
• Picture 4. Start with the word **then** and tell what she did in picture 4. **(Call on a child. Idea:** *Then she watered the tree.***)**

5. The vocabulary box shows words that you could use in your sentences.

watered	hole	dug	put

- Your turn: Write sentences for each picture. Pencils down when you're finished.
  (Observe children and give feedback.)
6. (Call on different children to read their whole paragraph. Praise good sentences. Tell how to fix up sentences with problems.)
7. (Collect papers. Mark errors in clarity, spelling and punctuation. During the next language period, pass back the corrected papers and present Exercise B.)

REWRITING

- (Return corrected papers to children.) You did a good job the first time you wrote about the girl. Now you're going to write a perfect paper. Rewrite the whole story from the beginning. Write it so it doesn't have any mistakes.
- (After children complete their final draft, post the papers [and illustrations] of the story.)

Extension Lesson 54

Materials: BLM 54. Lined paper.

Objective A: Write a paragraph based on four pictures.

Objective B: Rewrite the paragraph.

EXERCISE A
PARAGRAPH WRITING

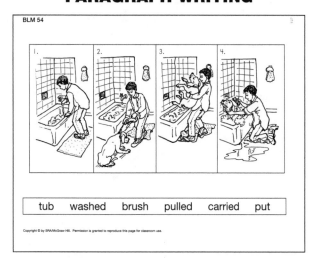

| tub | washed | brush | pulled | carried | put |

1. (Display or hand out BLM 54. Point to the pictures.)
   You're going to write a paragraph about what these pictures show.
2. You'll start with a good first sentence that tells what the boy did in these pictures.
   - What did the boy do in these pictures? (Call on a child. Idea: *Washed a dog.*) Yes, the boy washed a dog.
   - Write a good first sentence that tells about what the boy did. Remember to indent. Pencils down when you're finished.
   (Observe children and give feedback.)

- (Call on different children to read their first sentence.)
3. (Write on the board:)

> **First**
>
> **Then**

Now you're going to tell how the boy did that. The words on the board show the first word of each sentence. The sentence for picture 1 begins with the word **first.** The sentences for the next pictures start with the word **then.**

4. Picture 1. What did the boy do in that picture? (Call on a child. Idea: *Filled the tub with water.*)
   - Start with the word **first** and say a sentence for picture 1. (Call on a child. Idea: *First he filled the tub with water.*)
   - Picture 2. Start with the word **then** and say a sentence about picture 2. (Call on a child. Idea: *Then he pulled the dog to the bathtub.*)
   - Picture 3. Start with the word **then** and tell what he did in picture 3. (Call on a child. Idea: *Then he put the dog in the tub.*)
   - Picture 4. Start with the word **then** and tell what he did in picture 4. (Call on a child. Idea: *Then he washed the dog with a brush.*)

5. The vocabulary box shows words that you could use in your sentences.

tub	washed	brush
pulled	carried	put

- Your turn: Write sentences for each picture. Pencils down when you're finished.
  (Observe children and give feedback.)
4. (Call on different children to read their whole paragraph. Praise good sentences. Tell how to fix up sentences with problems.)
5. (Collect papers. Mark errors in clarity, spelling and punctuation. During the next language period, pass back the corrected papers and present Exercise B.)

REWRITING

- (Return corrected papers to children.) You did a good job the first time you wrote about the boy. Now you're going to write a perfect paper. Rewrite the whole story from the beginning. Write it so it doesn't have any mistakes.
- (After children complete their final draft, post the papers [and illustrations] of the story.)

Extension Lesson 55

Materials: BLM 55. Lined paper.

Objective A: Write a paragraph based on four pictures.

Objective B: Rewrite the paragraph.

EXERCISE A
PARAGRAPH WRITING

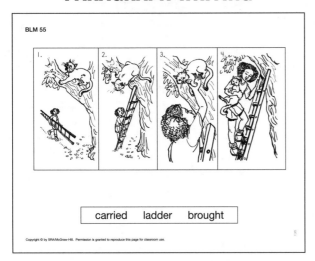

1. (Display or hand out BLM 55. Point to the pictures.)
   You're going to write a paragraph about what these pictures show.
2. You'll start with a good first sentence that tells what the girl did in these pictures.
   - What did the girl do in these pictures? (Call on a child. Ideas: *Rescued a cat. Brought a cat down from the tree.*)
   - Write the first sentence of your paragraph. Remember to indent. Pencils down when you're finished. (Observe children and give feedback.)
   - (Call on different children to read their first sentence.)

3. (Write on the board:)

First
Then

   Now you're going to tell how the girl did that. The words on the board show the first word of each sentence. The sentence for picture 1 begins with the word **first.** The sentences for the next pictures start with the word **then.**
4. Picture 1. What did the girl do in that picture? (Call on a child. Idea: *Carried a ladder over to the tree.*)
   - Start with the word **first** and say a sentence for picture 1. (Call on a child. Idea: *First she carried a ladder over to the tree.*)
   - Picture 2. Start with the word **then** and say a sentence about picture 2. (Call on a child. Idea: *Then she climbed up the ladder.*)
   - Picture 3. Start with the word **then** and tell what she did in picture 3. (Call on a child. Idea: *Then she grabbed the cat.*)
   - Picture 4. Start with the word **then** and tell what she did in picture 4. (Call on a child. Idea: *Then she carried the cat down the ladder.*)
5. The vocabulary box shows words that you could use in your sentences.

carried	ladder	brought

   - Your turn: Write sentences for each picture. Pencils down when you're finished. (Observe children and give feedback.)

6. (Call on different children to read their whole paragraph. Praise good sentences. Tell how to fix up sentences with problems.)

7. (Collect papers. Mark errors in clarity, spelling and punctuation. During the next language period, pass back the corrected papers and present Exercise B.)

REWRITING

- (Return corrected papers to children.) You did a good job the first time you wrote about the girl. Now you're going to write a perfect paper. Rewrite the whole story from the beginning. Write it so it doesn't have any mistakes.

- (After children complete their final draft, post the papers [and illustrations] of the story.)

Extension Lesson 56

> **Materials:** BLM 56. Lined paper.
> **Objective A:** **Write a passage to explain a 5-step process.**
> **Objective B:** Rewrite the passage.

EXERCISE A
PASSAGE WRITING

1. (Display or hand out BLM 56. Point to the pictures.)
   You're going to write a passage that tells how to make French toast.
   - (Write on the board:)

   ### Fill

   - Look at picture 1. It shows what you do first. You fill one cup with something. What goes in the cup? (Signal.) *Milk.*
   - Who can say a sentence that tells the first thing you do to make French toast? (Call on a child. Idea: *Fill a cup with milk.*)

2. (Write on the board:)

   ### Put

   - Look at picture 2. That picture shows where you put the milk. Where do you put it? (Call on a child. Idea: *In a bowl.*)
   - What else do you put in the bowl? (Call on a child. Idea: *Three eggs.*)
   - Who can make up a sentence that tells about putting the milk and eggs in the bowl? (Call on a child. Idea: *Put the milk and three eggs in a bowl.*)
   - Remember, you have to name the milk and the three eggs.

3. (Write on the board:)

   ### Mix

   - Look at picture 3. That picture shows what you do with the milk and the three eggs. What is that spoon doing? (Call on a child. Idea: *Mixing the eggs and the milk.*)
   - Who can make up a sentence that tells what you do with the milk and eggs? (Call on a child. Ideas: *Mix the milk and the eggs. Mix the milk and three eggs with a spoon.*)

4. (Write on the board:)

   ### Dip

   - Look at picture 4. The picture shows what you dip in the bowl. What do you dip? (Call on a child. Idea: *A slice of bread.*)

- Who can make up a sentence that tells what you dip in the bowl? (Call on a child. Ideas: *Dip bread in the bowl. Dip slices of bread in the bowl.*)
5. (Write on the board:)

Cook

- Look at picture 5. That shows the last thing you do. What is the French toast cooking in? (Call on a child. Idea: *A frying pan.*)
- Who can make up a sentence that tells how to cook the French toast? (Call on a child. Idea: *Cook the French toast in a frying pan.*)
6. You'll write directions for fixing French toast.
- (Point to title on BLM 56.) You start with a title: **Making French Toast.** Copy the title on the top line of your paper. Pencils down when you're finished.
  (Observe children and give feedback.)
7. (Point to vocabulary box.)

three	spoon	milk	bread
bowl	frying	slice	

- The vocabulary box shows words that you could use in your sentences.
- (Point to: **Fill** ▮▮▮▮▮▮▮▮▮.) The first word for each sentence is shown. Start with the word **fill** and write the first sentence. Pencils down when you're finished.
  (Observe children and give feedback.)
- (Call on different children to read their sentences. Praise good sentences. Tell children who wrote inadequate sentences how to change them.)
8. Start with the word **put** and write the second sentence. Pencils down when you're finished.
  (Observe children and give feedback.)

- (Call on different children to read their sentences. Praise good sentences. Tell children who wrote inadequate sentences how to change them.)
9. Start with the word **mix** and write the third sentence. Pencils down when you're finished.
  (Observe children and give feedback.)
- (Call on different children to read their sentences. Praise good sentences. Tell children who wrote inadequate sentences how to change them.)
10. Start with the word **dip** and write the fourth sentence. Pencils down when you're finished.
  (Observe children and give feedback.)
- (Call on different children to read their sentences. Praise good sentences. Tell children who wrote inadequate sentences how to change them.)
11. Start with the word **cook** and write the last sentence. Pencils down when you're finished.
  (Observe children and give feedback.)
- (Call on different children to read their sentences. Praise good sentences. Tell children who wrote inadequate sentences how to change them.)
12. (Collect papers. Mark errors in clarity, spelling and punctuation. During the next language period, pass back the corrected papers and present Exercise B.)

EXERCISE B
REWRITING

- (Return corrected papers to children.) You did a good job the first time you wrote about making French toast. Now you're going to write a perfect paper. Rewrite the directions from the beginning. Write them so they don't have any mistakes.
- (After children complete their final draft, post the papers [and illustrations] of the directions.)

Extension Lesson

Materials: Lined paper. Illustrating materials.

Objective A: **Write a report of a personal experience.**

Objective B: **Finish the report by rewriting and illustrating.**

EXERCISE A

REPORTING ON PERSONAL EXPERIENCE

1. You're going to write about the last time you went to the doctor. First we'll talk about what you did.
2. (Write on the board:)

> ### WHEN

- Listen: The first thing you'll tell about is **when** you went to the doctor. Was it in the summer? Do you remember the year it was? Was it just before summer vacation, or was it in the middle of winter? Were you five years old or six years old? Start with the words **the last time I went to the doctor** and tell when you went there.

(Call on different children. Praise children who start with the words *the last time I went to the doctor* and who give some indication of when.)

> (To correct: If children start to tell more than **when,** stop them and remind them that they are just telling **when.**)

3. (Write on the board:)

> ### WHY

- Listen: After you tell about **when,** you'll tell about **why** you went to the doctor. Start with the words **I went to the doctor because** and tell why you went there. Did you have a cold? Did you have a sore throat? Did you have a checkup? Did you have a broken arm? Tell the reason.

(Call on different children. Praise children who start with the words *I went to the doctor because* and who tell the reason.)

> (To correct: If children tell more than **why** they went to the doctor, stop them and remind them that they are simply telling **why** they went to the doctor.)

4. (Write on the board:)

> ### WHAT HAPPENED

- After you tell why you went to the doctor, tell what happened. Tell how you felt when you went in. Tell what the doctor did. Did it hurt? Did you take some pills? Did you get a shot? Then tell how you felt when you left.
- Listen again: Tell how you felt when you went in. Tell what the doctor did and what you did. Then tell how you felt when you left.

(Call on different children. Praise accounts that give details about what happened.)

5. (Write on the board:)

The Last Time I Went to the Doctor

• Now you're going to write your report on lined paper. Copy the title on the top line of your paper. Pencils down when you've done that much.
   (Observe children and give feedback.)

6. First you'll tell when. Start with the words **I went to the doctor** and write one or more sentences that tell **when** that happened. Remember to indent. Pencils down when you're finished.
   (Observe children and give feedback.)

7. (Write on the board:)

I went to the doctor because

• Now you're going to tell why you went there. Start with the words **I went to the doctor because** and tell why you went there. Tell what the reason was. Tell how you felt after you went to the doctor. You can write more than one sentence. Pencils down when you're finished.
   (Observe children and give feedback.)

8. Now you're going to write about what happened. Remember, tell how you felt when you went in, what the doctor did and said and how you felt when you went out. Pencils down when you're finished.
   (Observe children and give feedback.)

9. Now you can write anything to tell what happened later on. Tell if you got better or if you still had the problem. Pencils down when you're finished.
   (Observe children and give feedback.)

10. (Call on different children to read their entire account. Give feedback about good parts and parts that have problems.)

11. (Collect papers and give feedback for changes. Mark sentences that do not have ending marks. Mark parts that do not tell what they are supposed to tell.)

FINISHING A REPORT

• (Children are later to revise their papers and incorporate the changes you indicated.)

• (After revising their reports, have them illustrate their reports with a picture that shows them at the doctor's office. They may write labels [doctor, nurse, me] for the people in the picture.)

Extension Lesson 58

> **Materials:** Lined paper. Illustrating materials.
> **Objective A:** Write a report of a personal experience.
> **Objective B:** Finish the report by rewriting and illustrating.

EXERCISE A

REPORTING ON PERSONAL EXPERIENCE

1. You're going to write about a time you got really scared. First we'll talk about it.
2. (Write on the board:)

> **WHEN**

- Listen: The first thing you'll tell about is **when** it happened. Was it in the summer or was it in the middle of winter? Do you remember the year it was? Do you remember how old you were? Start with the words **something really scared me** and tell when it happened.
  (Call on different children. Praise children who start with the words *something really scared me* and who give some indication of when.)
  > (To correct: If children start to tell more than **when,** stop them and remind them that they are just telling **when.**)

3. (Write on the board:)

> **WHERE**

- The next thing you'll tell is **where** it happened. Were you at home or somewhere else? Were you in a car or a house, or were you on your bike? Where were you? Start with the words **I was** and tell where you were.
  (Call on different children. Praise children who start with the words *I was* and that tell where the child was.)

4. (Write on the board:)

> **WHY**

- Listen: After you tell about where you were, tell **why** you were there. What were you doing? What did you plan to do? Start with the words **I was there because** and tell why you were there.
  (Call on different children. Praise children who start with the words *I was there because* and who tell the reason.)
  > (To correct: If children tell more than **why** they were there, stop them and remind them that they are simply telling **why** they were there.)

5. (Write on the board:)

WHAT HAPPENED

- After you tell why you were at the place, tell what happened. Tell what happened to scare you. Tell what you did after you were scared. Tell the other important things that went on. Did anybody get hurt? Did you get away from what scared you? Tell what happened.
  (Call on different children. Praise accounts that give details about what happened.)
6. (Write on the board:)

A Time I Was Really Scared

- Now you're going to write your report on lined paper. Copy the title on the top line of your paper. Pencils down when you've done that much.
  (Observe children and give feedback.)
7. First you'll tell **when.** Start with the words **something really scared me** and tell when. Write one or more sentences. Remember to indent. Pencils down when you're finished.
  (Observe children and give feedback.)
8. (Write on the board:)

WHERE

- Now you're going to tell where you were. Start with the words **I was** and tell where you were. If you were with somebody else, you can also tell who was with you. Pencils down when you've written about where you were.
  (Observe children and give feedback.)

9. Now you're going to tell why you were there. Start with the words **I was there because** and tell why you were there. Tell what you planned to do there before something scared you. Pencils down when you're finished.
  (Observe children and give feedback.)
10. Now you can write about what happened. Remember, tell how you felt before you were scared. Tell what happened to scare you. Tell how you felt and what you did after you were scared. Pencils down when you're finished.
  (Observe children and give feedback.)
11. Now you can write an ending. You can tell what happened later on. Pencils down when you're finished.
  (Observe children and give feedback.)
12. (Call on different children to read their entire account. Give feedback about good parts and parts that have problems.)
13. (Collect papers and give feedback for changes. Mark sentences that do not have ending marks. Mark parts that do not tell what they are supposed to tell.)

EXERCISE B
FINISHING A REPORT

- (Children are later to revise their papers and incorporate the changes you indicated.)
- (After revising their reports, have them illustrate their reports with a picture that shows them being scared. They may write labels for the people or things in the picture.)

Extension Lesson 59

Materials:	Lined paper. Illustrating materials.

Materials: Lined paper. Illustrating materials.
Objective A: Write a report of a personal experience.
Objective B: Finish the report by rewriting and illustrating.

EXERCISE A

REPORTING ON PERSONAL EXPERIENCE

1. You're going to write about a time you did something that was really **good.** That's something you're really proud you did. First we'll talk about it.
2. (Write on the board:)

WHEN

- Listen: The first thing you'll tell about is when it happened. Was it in the summer or was it in the middle of winter? Do you remember the year it was? Do you remember how old you were? Start with the words **I did something really good** and tell when it happened.
(Call on different children. Praise children who start with the words *I did something really good* and who give some indication of when.)
  (To correct: If children start to tell more than **when,** stop them and remind them that they are just telling **when.**)

3. (Write on the board:)

WHERE

- The next thing you'll tell is where it happened. Were you at home or somewhere else? Were you in a car or a house, or were you on your bike? Where were you? Start with the words **I was** and tell where you were. You can also tell who you were with.
(Call on different children. Praise accounts that start with the words *I was* and that tell where the child was and possibly who was with the child.)
4. (Write on the board:)

WHY

- Listen: After you tell about where you were, tell **why** you were there. What were you doing? What did you plan to do? Start with the words **I was there because** and tell why you were there.
(Call on different children. Praise children who start with the words *I was there because* and who tell the reason.)
  (To correct: If children tell more than **why** they were there, stop them and remind them that they are simply telling **why** they were there.)

5. (Write on the board:)

WHAT HAPPENED

- After you tell why you were at the place, tell what happened. Tell what you did that was good. Tell all the important things that went on. Tell what you did that was good and why you were proud of what you did. If you helped somebody else, tell how that person felt and what that person said.
(Call on different children. Praise accounts that give details about what happened.)

6. (Write on the board:)

Something Really Good

- Now you're going to write your report on lined paper. Copy the title on the top line of your paper. Pencils down when you've done that much.
(Observe children and give feedback.)

7. First you'll tell **when.** Start with the words **I did something really good** and tell when it happened. Write one or more sentences. Remember to indent. Pencils down when you're finished.
(Observe children and give feedback.)

8. Now you're going to tell where you were. Start with the words **I was** and tell where you were. If you were with somebody else, you can also tell who was with you. Pencils down when you've written about where you were.
(Observe children and give feedback.)

9. Now you're going to tell why you were there. Start with the words **I was there because** and tell why you were there. Tell what you planned to do there. Pencils down when you're finished.
(Observe children and give feedback.)

10. Now you're going to write about what you did that was really good. Remember, tell what you did that was really good and tell why it was good. Tell how you felt. If you helped somebody else, tell what that person said. Pencils down when you're finished.
(Observe children and give feedback.)

11. Now you can write an ending. You can tell what happened later on. Pencils down when you're finished.
(Observe children and give feedback.)

12. **(Call on different children to read their entire account. Give feedback about good parts and parts that have problems.)**

13. **(Collect papers and give feedback for changes. Mark sentences that do not have ending marks. Mark parts that do not tell what they are supposed to tell.)**

EXERCISE B
FINISHING A REPORT

- **(Children are later to revise their papers and incorporate the changes you indicated.)**
- **(After revising their reports, have them illustrate their reports with a picture that shows them doing something good. They may write labels for the people or things in the picture.)**

Extension Lesson 60

Materials: Lined paper. Illustrating materials.

Objective A: Write a report of a personal experience.

Objective B: Finish the report by rewriting and illustrating.

EXERCISE A
REPORTING ON PERSONAL EXPERIENCE

1. You're going to write about a time somebody did something that made you really happy. Maybe it happened at Christmas or on your birthday when you got a present you didn't expect but that you really wanted. Maybe it was in the summer when somebody took you to a place that made you really happy. Maybe it was when somebody did something to help you out and you really liked what the person did.

2. (Write on the board:)

> ### Something That Made Me Happy

- Here's the title to your paragraph. Copy the title.

3. (Write on the board:)

> ### WHO

- Listen: The first thing you'll write about is who made you happy. If your mother made you happy, start with the words **my mother** and say **my mother made me happy.** If a friend named Don made you happy, start with the words **my friend Don** and say **my friend Don made me happy.** Write your first sentence. Remember to indent. (Observe children and give feedback.)
- (Call on different children to read their first sentence. Praise good sentences.)

4. (Write on the board:)

> ### WHERE

- The next thing you'll write is where it happened. Were you at home or somewhere else? Were you in a car or a house, or were you on your bike? Where were you? Start with the words **I was** and write about where you were. You can also tell who you were with. Pencils down when you're finished. (Observe children and give feedback.)
- (Call on different children. Praise accounts that start with the words *I was* and that tell where the child was and possibly who was with the child.)

5. (Write on the board:)

WHEN

- Now you'll write a sentence that tells when it happened. You can write a sentence that starts with **it was: It was Christmas** or **it was my sixth birthday** or **it was last summer.** Write your sentence that tells when. Pencils down when you're finished.

  (Observe children and give feedback.)
- (Call on different children. Praise children who start with the words *It was* and tell when.)

6. (Write on the board:)

WHAT HAPPENED

- Tell what the person did. Tell how you felt when the person did that. Pencils down when you're finished.

  (Observe children and give feedback.)
- (Call on different children. Praise accounts that give details about what happened and how the child felt.)

7. Now you can write an ending. You can tell what happened later on. You can also tell how you feel about the person who did the thing that made you so happy. Pencils down when you're finished.

  (Observe children and give feedback.)

8. (Call on different children to read their entire account. Give feedback about good parts and parts that have problems.)

9. (Collect papers and give feedback for changes. Mark sentences that do not have ending marks. Mark parts that do not tell what they are supposed to tell.)

FINISHING A REPORT

- (Children are later to revise their papers and incorporate the changes you indicated.)
- (After revising their reports, have them illustrate their reports with a picture that shows what the other person was doing that made the child happy. Children may write labels for the people or things in the picture.)

Reproducible Blackline Masters

Table of Contents

The cat was sitting in
the grass.
The dog ███████████████.

	The dog was sitting on the
	floor.
	The cat ████████████.

	A boy was riding a bike.
	A girl ██████████████████ .

The girl rode an elephant.
The boy ▬▬▬▬▬▬▬▬▬▬▬▬▬.

The boy read a paper.

	The girl was standing on
	a chair.
	████████████████████████ .

BLM 7

Copyright © by SRA/McGraw-Hill. Permission is granted to reproduce this page for classroom use.

A cat was sleeping on the chair.

90

The girl was drawing a picture.

milk poured some banana peeled

an apple   an orange   peeled   ate

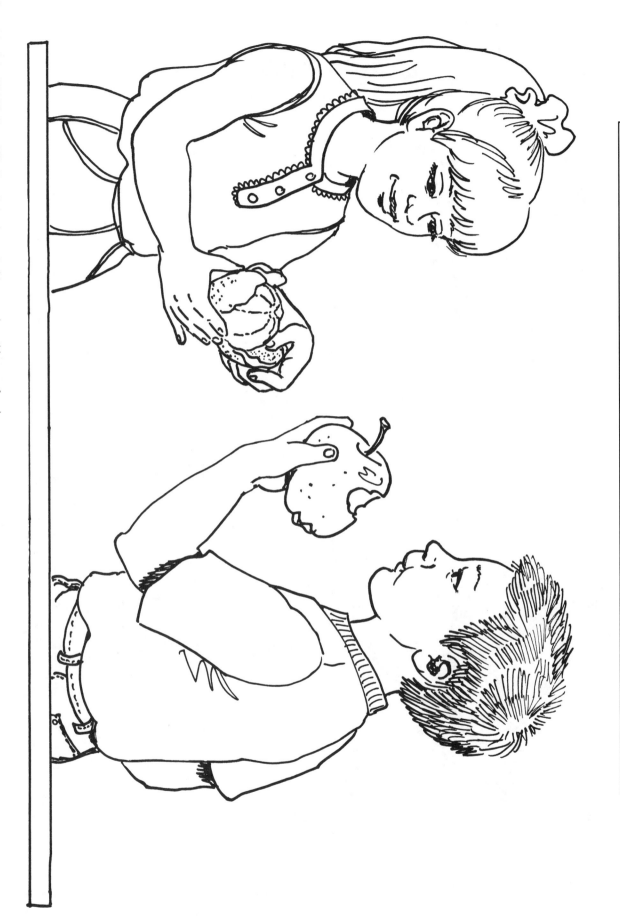

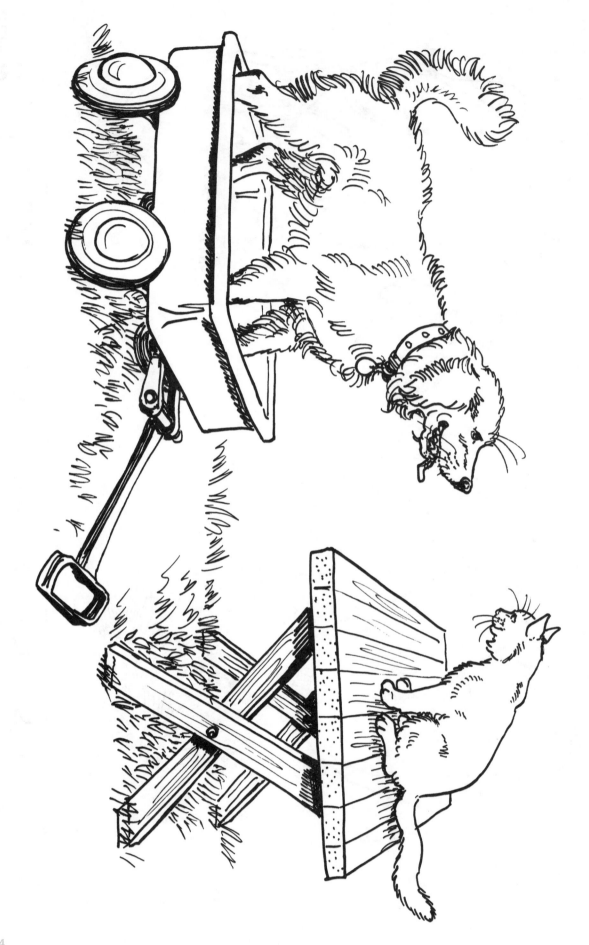

standing   sitting   table   wagon

climbed   chewed   bone

popcorn   reading   eating

next box chair

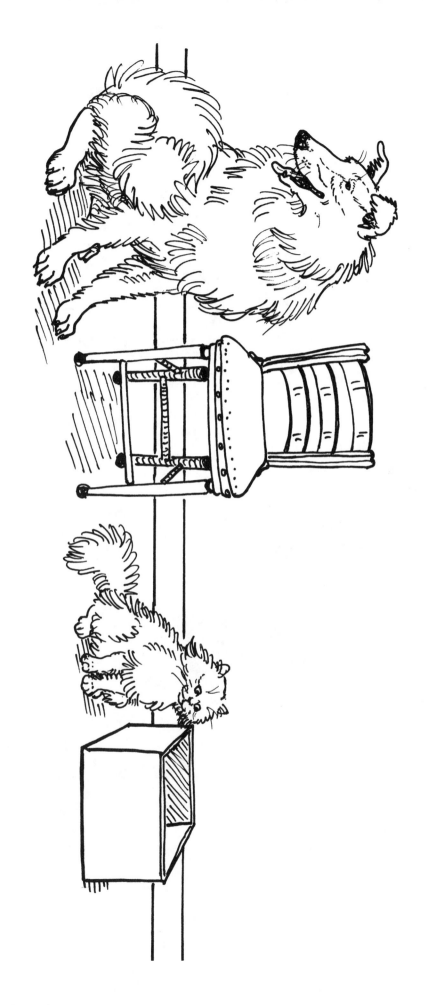

sawed   painted   woman   board

skipped   catch   played   rope

chair   woman   sitting   painting

rode   horse   bike   girl

mopped   washed   dishes   floor

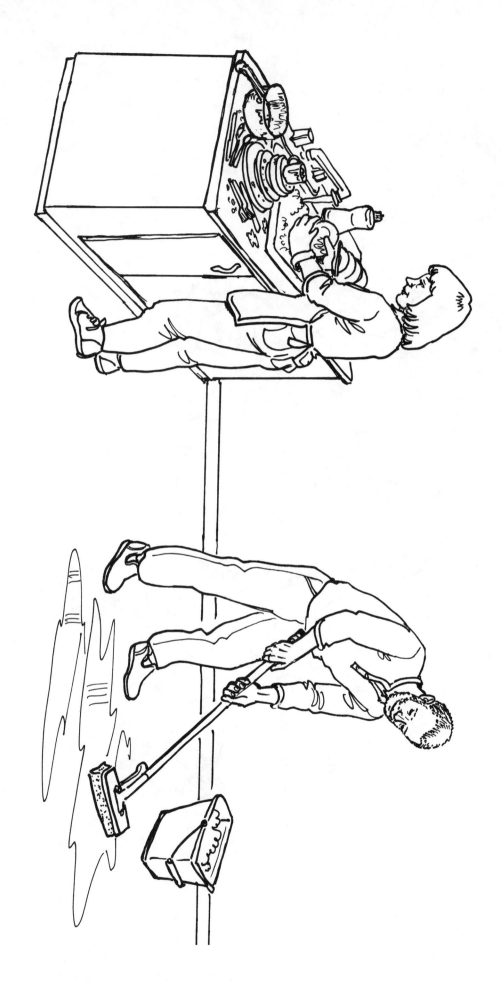

| its | gray | scratched | chased | rabbit | ear |

ceiling short tall painting

ate spotted corn white goat grass

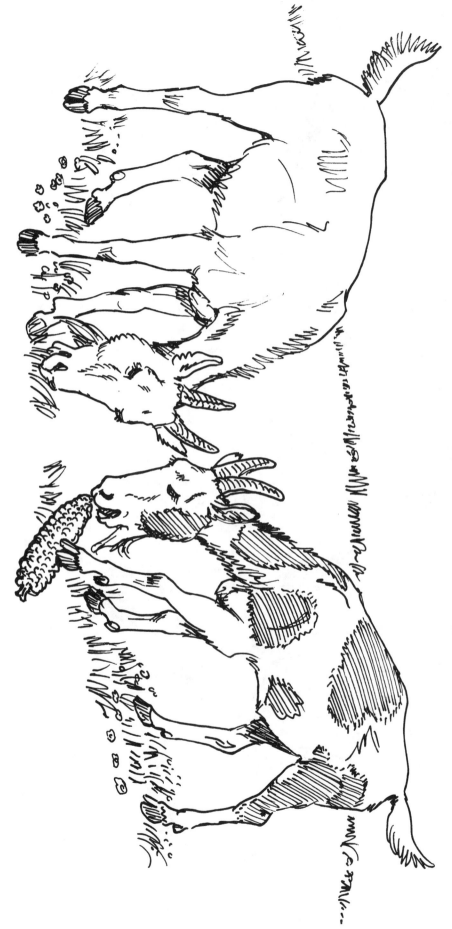

young   leaves   chopped   raked

spotted   kitten   playing   sleeping   white

were carrying box woman young bike

chased   spotted   white

younger boat fishing rowing

drawing   skipping   younger   older   girl

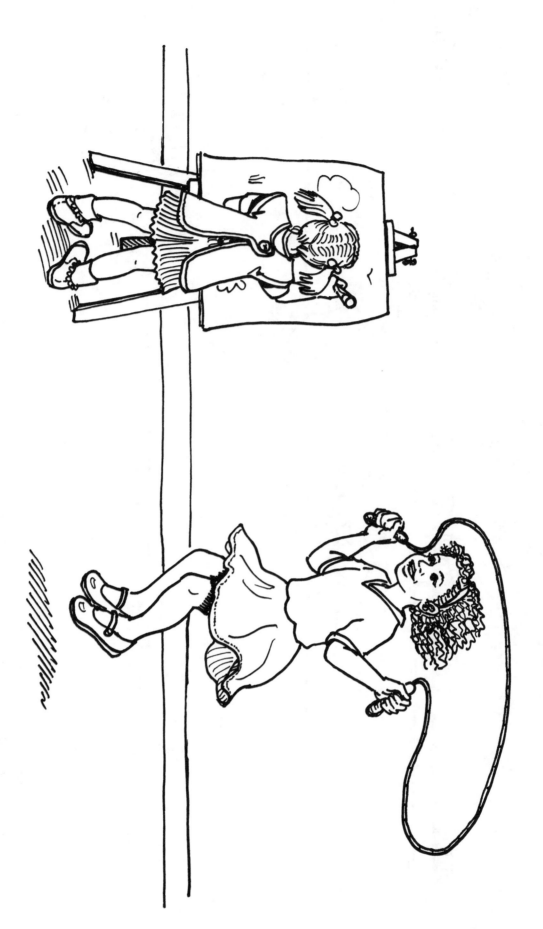

swimming   eating   were   ice cream

sleeping   reading   women   were

horses   running   goats   eating

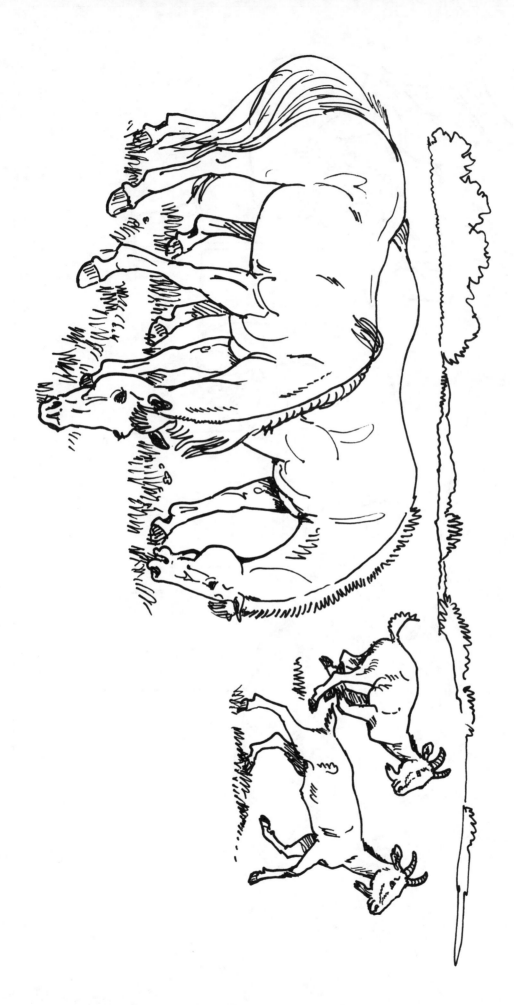

women   leaves   grass   mowed   younger

dishes   younger   table   washed   set

watching   were   TV

117

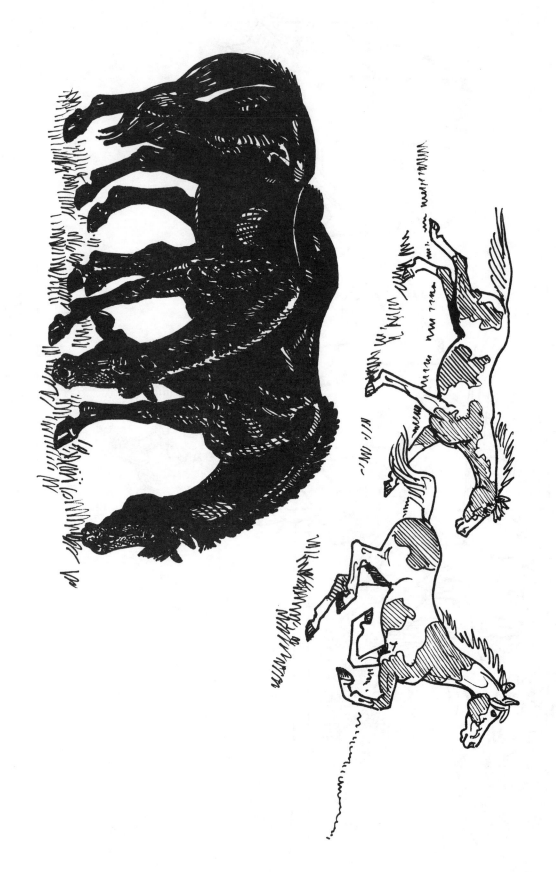

horses grass were spotted eating running

climbed

floor   washed   swept   windows   women

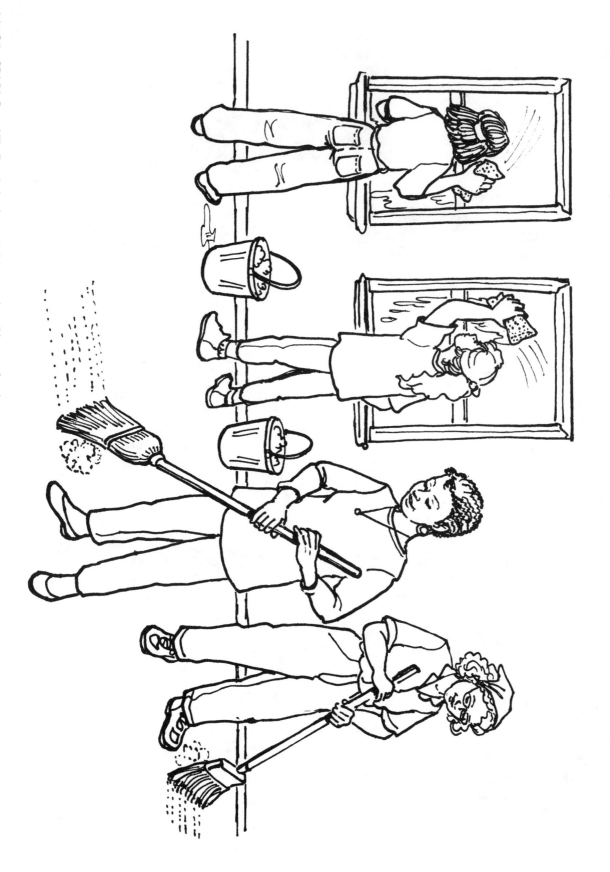

washed   boys

squirrels   sidewalk

frying   bowl   eating   were

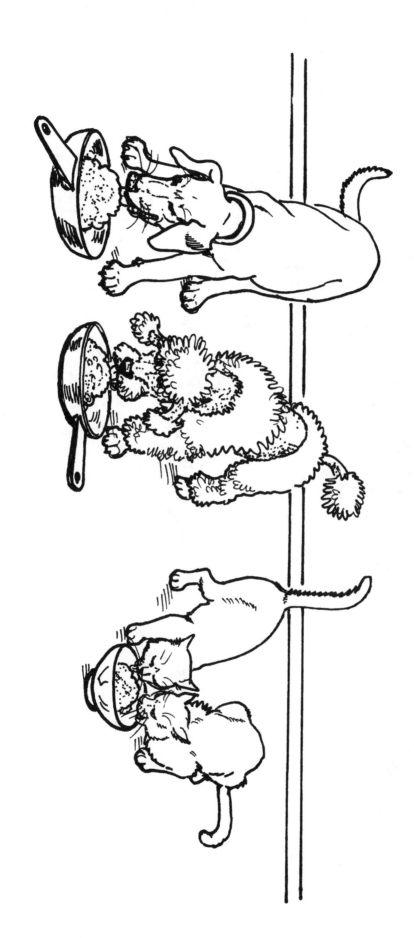

rabbits   frying   bowls   ate

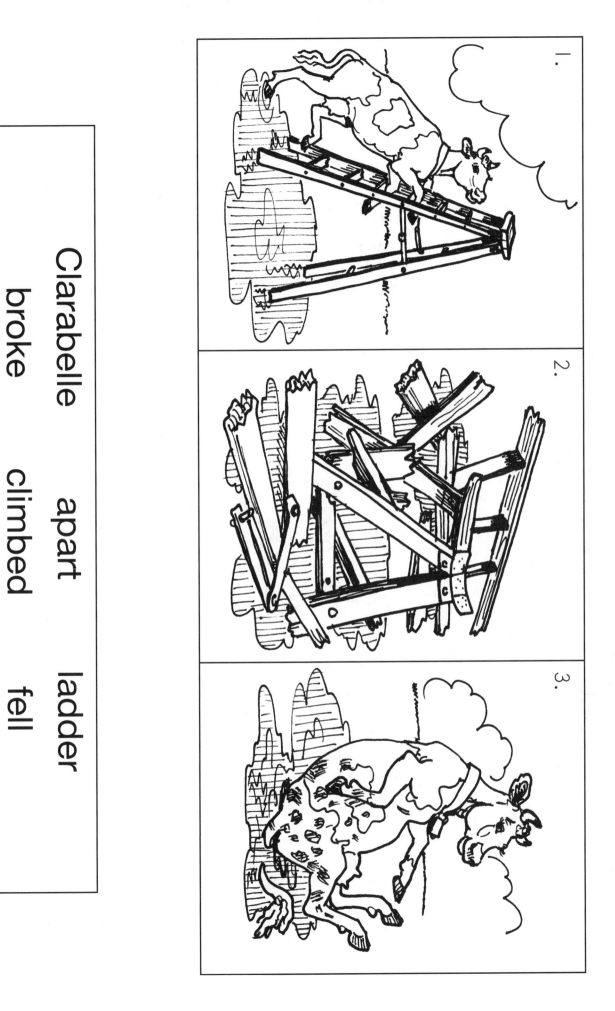

Clarabelle   apart   ladder

broke   climbed   fell

clothes   picked   made

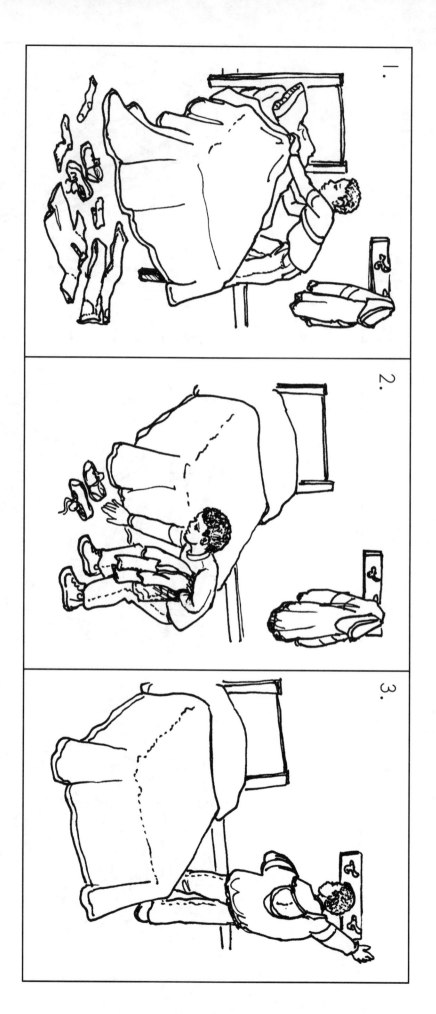

front   bigger   porch   two   window

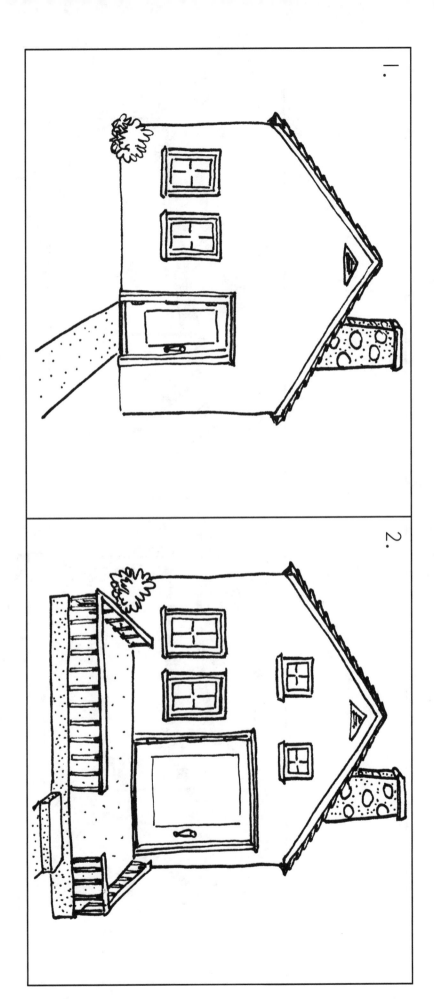

1.

2.

1.

2.

pillow   rose   blanket   another

1.

2.

around   bow   ribbon   wrapping paper

A bird fell out of a tree. It landed on the ground. A boy picked up the bird. He took it home.

women   leaves   working   were

younger   mowing   raking

are   everybody   something   washing   is

animals were bowl
containers frying pan eating

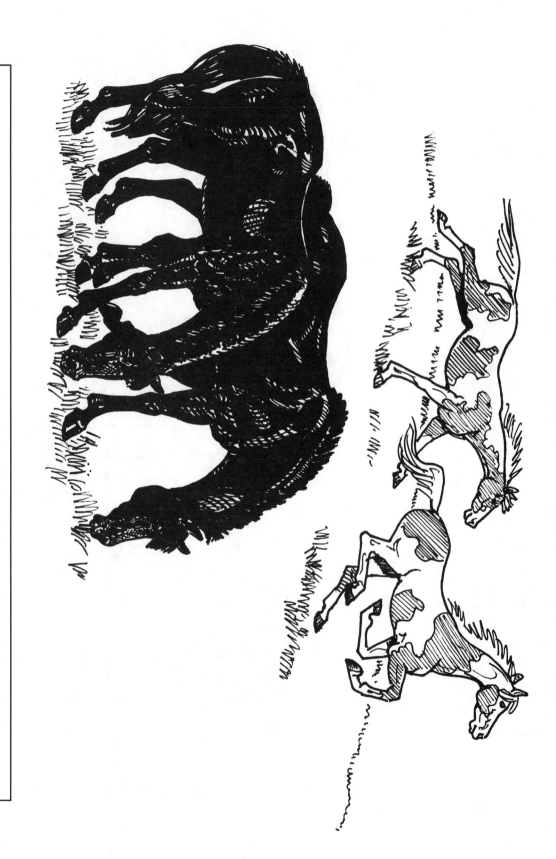

horses   were   field   eating   running

woman   each   carried   something   younger

watered   hole   dug   put

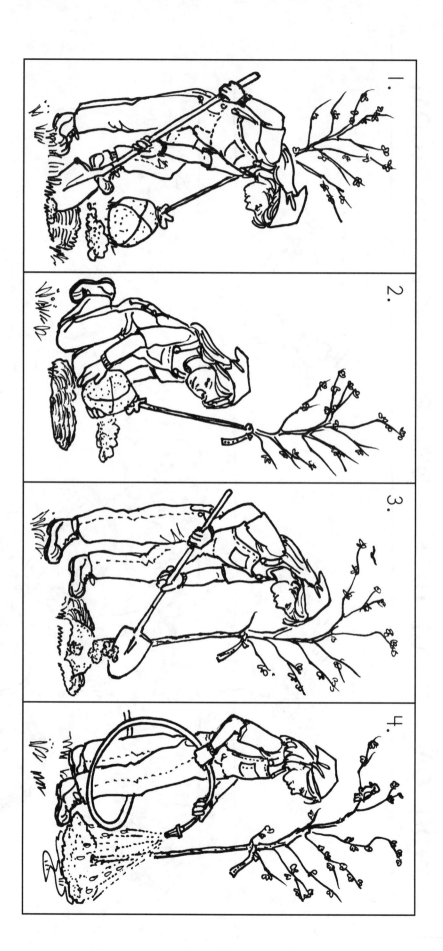

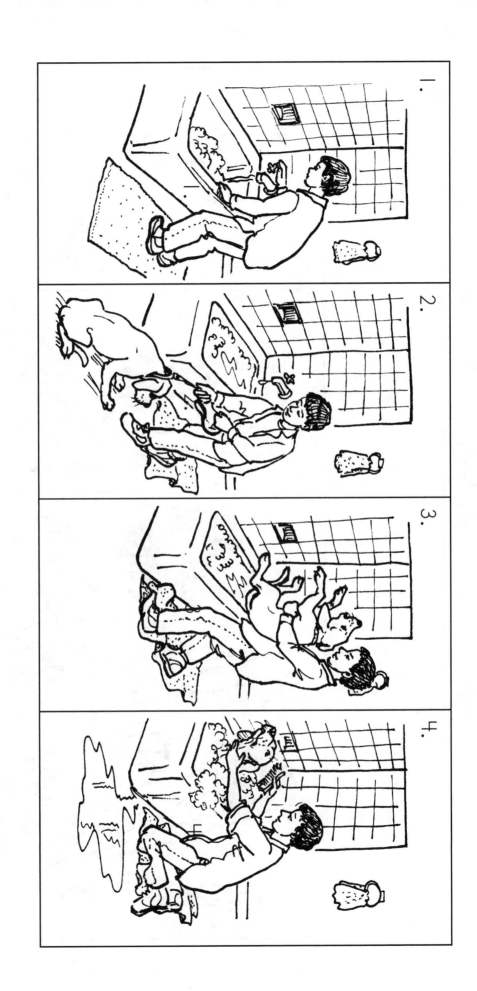

tub   washed   brush   pulled   carried   put

carried   ladder   brought

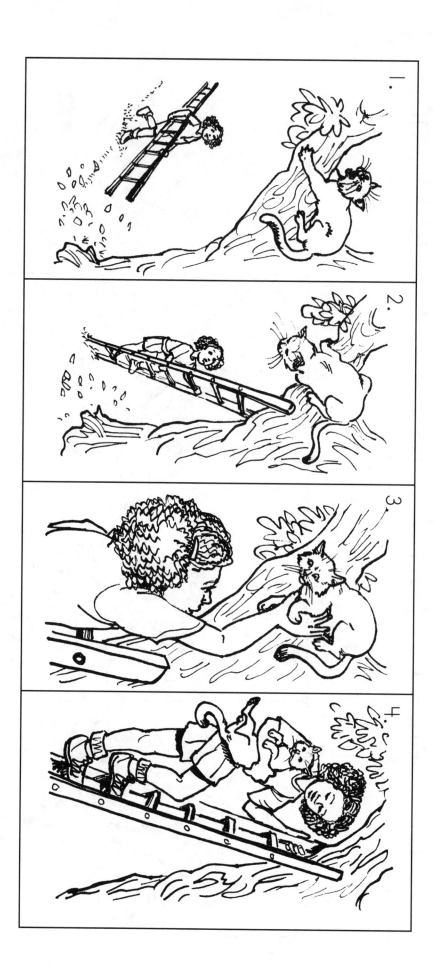

Making French Toast

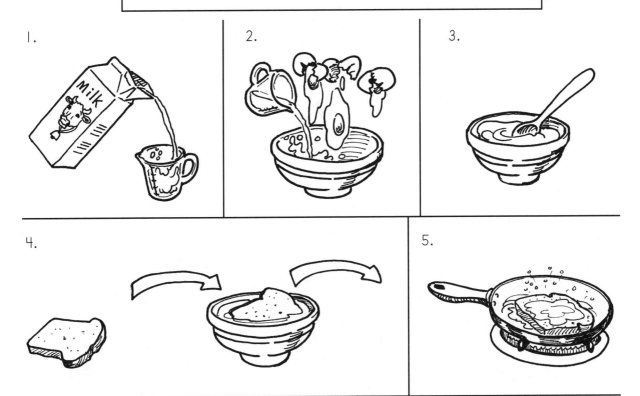

1.
2.
3.
4.
5.

three   spoon
milk   bread
bowl   frying
slice

	Fill ▮▮▮▮ .
	Put ▮▮▮▮ .
	Mix ▮▮▮▮ .
	Dip ▮▮▮▮ .
	Cook ▮▮▮▮ .